Fascinating Bible Studies on Every Parable

Dr. William H. Marty

BETHANY HOUSE
a division of Baker Publishing Group
Minneapolis, Minnesota

© 2020 by William H. Marty

Published by Bethany House Publishers
11400 Hampshire Avenue South
Bloomington, Minnesota 55438
www.bethanyhouse.com

Bethany House Publishers is a division of
Baker Publishing Group, Grand Rapids, Michigan

Printed in the United States of America

Library of Congress Cataloging-in-Publication Data
Names: Marty, William Henry, author.
Title: Fascinating bible studies on every parable / Dr. William H. Marty.
Description: Minneapolis, Minnesota : Bethany House Publishers, [2020]
Identifiers: LCCN 2020000567 | ISBN 9780764232442 (trade paperback) | ISBN 9781493424894 (ebook)
Subjects: LCSH: Bible—Parables—Textbooks. | Bible—Parables—Criticism, interpretation, etc.
Classification: LCC BS680.P3 M37 2020 | DDC 226.8/06—dc23
LC record available at https://lccn.loc.gov/2020000567

Cover design by LOOK Design Studio

20 21 22 23 24 25 26   7 6 5 4 3 2 1

Contents

The Ethics of the Kingdom

Introduction

One of the reasons Jesus is considered a Master Teacher was his extensive use of parables. He used them to teach large and small crowds like his disciples and to debate religious leaders.

Why did Jesus teach in parables? He used parables to draw his audience into the story. Once they identified with the characters, he would make a point, usually with an unexpected development. Though the stories were from everyday life, they were not always understood, even by his disciples. Jesus had to explain. "With many similar parables Jesus spoke the word to them, as much as they could understand. He did not say anything to them without using a parable. But when he was alone with his own disciples, he explained everything" (Mark 4:33–34).

While this book is mostly about Jesus' parables, I have also included two parables from the Old Testament. The story of the trees and the Shechemites could be considered a fable because inanimate objects (trees) are assigned traits of the living, but it is a parable in that the story focuses on one main point. Also, Nathan used a parable of a rich man and a poor man to rebuke David for his sin with Bathsheba. In addition to parables in the Old Testament, the rabbis of Jesus' time taught in parables, so Jesus was using a method that would have been familiar to his audience. But Jesus' use of parables was somewhat unique because no one had used parables as extensively as he did in his teaching about the kingdom.

While writing these studies, I occasionally interacted with my brother-in-law about some of the parables. His response was often, "I never did understand what Jesus meant." The purpose of this book is to help you understand Jesus' parables—what he intended to teach and the response he expected—and then to suggest how we can apply his parables today.

Each study begins with an introduction followed by information on the historical and cultural setting of the parable. It is important to place each parable within the ministry of Jesus and to understand the cultural aspects of the story. Though it is difficult to categorize Jesus' parables because of the different occasions and varieties of the stories, I have attempted to organize them into two broad categories: 1) the nature of the kingdom and 2) the ethics of the kingdom.

The Nature of the Kingdom

When Jesus first began speaking in parables, he called them "mysteries." This meant that Jesus was revealing new truths about the kingdom—truths that had not been revealed in the Old Testament. Jesus declared that with his coming, the kingdom had arrived (the inauguration of the kingdom), the kingdom would advance supernaturally, the kingdom was of incomparable value, and the kingdom would be consummated at the end of the age ("already" but "not yet").

The Ethics of the Kingdom

The parables in this category answer the question that the late Francis Schaeffer asked and answered in his book *How Should We Then Live?* In the Sermon on the Mount, Jesus introduced "a higher calling" for subjects of the kingdom when he declared, "Unless your righteousness surpasses that of the scribes and Pharisees, you will not enter the kingdom of heaven" (Matthew 5:20 NASB). Parables in this section clarify what it means to be a devoted follower of Christ (discipleship); they introduce the shocking theme of reversal; and they warn of the tragic and irreversible fate of those who reject Jesus. Others give truths about prayer, assuring us that God is a loving Father who will not disappoint. Some, like the workers in the vineyard and the prodigal son, emphasize God's amazing grace and his unconditional love. The section concludes with a focus on fruitfulness, which includes the parable of the barren fig and Jesus' teaching about the vine and the branches. In my opinion, the latter is an extended metaphor, not a parable, but I have included it because of its importance for becoming and remaining a fruitful follower of Christ.

Why Do You Speak to the People in Parables?

When Jesus began teaching in parables, his disciples didn't understand. After the parable of the sower, they asked, "Why?" His answer is somewhat puzzling. He said,

> "The secret of the kingdom has been given to you. But to those on the outside everything is said in parables so that,
>> 'They may be ever hearing but never perceiving,
>> and ever hearing but never understanding;
>> otherwise they might turn and be forgiven!'"
>
> Mark 4:11–12

It seems as if Jesus taught in parables to deliberately conceal kingdom truths, at least from his detractors—those he refers to as "outsiders." Matthew gives additional information on Jesus' response with a longer quote from Isaiah. In Matthew, the failure to understand is due to the hardness of the hearts of the hearers rather than the intention of Jesus to prevent "outsiders" from understanding. Mark and Matthew give two different perspectives on the purpose of parables—Mark gives the divine and Matthew the human. In Matthew, the parable of the sower and six other parables come after Jesus faced vicious opposition and the charge that his power over demons was from Satan. Jesus warned his opponents that their deliberate and stubborn unbelief was an unpardonable sin (Matthew 12:1–37). The reason outsiders could not understand Jesus' parabolic teaching is because they didn't want to understand; they had hardened their hearts. Mark, however, gives God's perspective. Because Jesus' opponents, primarily the religious leaders, had deliberately hardened their hearts, God had hardened their hearts. They couldn't understand Jesus' teaching in parables because they didn't want to understand, thus God made it impossible for them to understand. They had committed "the unpardonable sin," and put themselves under divine judgment.

Only for Insiders

Since you are reading this book, I will assume you are what Jesus calls an "insider." You want to understand the "secrets of the kingdom" (Matthew 13:11).

The NLT and other contemporary translations and paraphrases have translated the word *mysteries* as "secrets." When we think of a mystery, we imagine something related to a crime or something that is strange and unknown. When we think of a secret, we think of information that is known only by a few people. Both of these terms are somewhat helpful for understanding what Jesus meant when he referred to "mysteries of the kingdom," but the biblical usage of the term *mystery* and the nature of the kingdom will help us to better understand the stories Jesus told.

Mystery

Mystery refers to truths hidden in the counsel of God that could not be known unless God revealed them. The classic example in the Old Testament is the revelation of Nebuchadnezzar's dream to Daniel. The king had a dream that none of his counselors could explain. He threatens to kill all his advisors, including Daniel and his friends, if they didn't interpret it. When Daniel and his friends prayed, the Lord revealed to Daniel the meaning (mystery) of the dream (Daniel 2:1–49).

Paul uses *mystery* nearly two dozen times in his epistles to refer to new revelations about Christ and various aspects of the Christian faith. John uses *mystery* to refer to the fulfillment of God's eschatological (future) plan as fulfilled in the book of Revelation. These are beyond the scope of this book, but all of the uses refer to the making known of divine truths that would have otherwise remained secret.

When his disciples asked why he spoke in parables, Jesus replied, "Because the knowledge of the secrets [literally, *mysteries*] of the kingdom of heaven has been given to you, but not to them" (Matthew 13:11). Jesus was referring to new truths about the kingdom of God—truths that had not been revealed in the Old Testament. For example, in the parable of the growing seed, Jesus reveals that the coming and advance of the kingdom is a secret process and not a sudden and spectacular event as envisioned in the Old Testament (cf. Mark 4:26–29 and Daniel 7:13–14, 26–27).

The Jesus Revolution

I don't particularly like rebels, but I must confess that I have been accused of being somewhat of a rebel. And some of my former students are rebels for Jesus. They have gone to places and started ministries that can only be described as revolutionary. One of my former students was asked to leave (expelled) from two countries for attempting to proclaim the gospel. He and his family are now missionaries in a third country that is not hostile to Christianity. Jesus was a rebel. His message about the kingdom was revolutionary. He wasn't expelled from Palestine; he was crucified for his revolutionary ideology.

In his insightful book *The Parables of Jesus*, David Wenham uses the concept of a "revolution" to describe Jesus' teaching about the kingdom of God (see chapter 2, "Setting the Scene: Jesus' Revolution"). I think the concept of "revolution" gives us a more accurate understanding of Jesus' inauguration of the kingdom. Wenham explains:

> To paraphrase "kingdom of God" with the phrase "revolution of God" may help us appreciate something of the excitement of Jesus' message. He was announcing a dramatic forceful change in society to people who—unlike many in our complacent modern world—really longed for such a change: God was at last intervening to put things right.[1]

Though the Old Testament, especially the prophets, looked forward to God intervening in history, Jesus' revolution was different than expected. Most anticipated the overthrow of the Romans and the establishment of a renewed Davidic kingdom (see 2 Samuel 7:1–29), but instead of a political/military empire to overthrow Roman rule, Jesus came to overthrow the kingdom of Satan. Jesus' kingdom was far greater than what Israel imagined. It was cosmic in scope, and spiritual: "For he has rescued us from the dominion of darkness and brought us into the kingdom of the Son he loves, in whom we have redemption, the forgiveness of sins" (Colossians 1:13–14). Though primarily spiritual in the present, Jesus' revolution anticipates the restoration of all creation that has been ruined by sin and Satan. We see a preview of Isaiah's new heavens and earth in Jesus' miracles (Isaiah 65:17–25).

Three examples of the "Jesus Revolution"

When his friends brought a paralyzed man to Jesus, Jesus initially forgave his sins. This infuriated the religious elite. They charged Jesus with blasphemy: "Who can forgive sins but God alone?" Jesus responded with a question: "Which is easier, to forgive sins or to heal?" He then healed the man as evidence of his divine authority to do both. Those present were amazed. They had never seen anything like this. This twofold miracle was a preview of both Jesus' present and future ministry when there would be no more sin and pain (Revelation 21:3–4). Jesus healed people of their diseases, but he did not heal everyone. His miracles were evidence that the revolution had come but was not complete.

Jesus also demonstrated his authority over nature. When the disciples were threatened by a violent storm on the Sea of Galilee, Jesus calmed the wild wind and waves with a single command: "Be still!" The disciples were bewildered and asked, "Who is this? Even the wind and the waves obey him!" (Mark 4:39–41). Though the popular application of this miracle is to Jesus calming the storms of life, I both agree and disagree. I believe this is a preview of when Jesus will restore all creation that has been corrupted by sin and Satan. It is evidenced in the command of Jesus. He gave the same command to the wind and waves that he did to the demon-possessed man in the synagogue at Capernaum (see Mark 1:25).

A third aspect of the Jesus revolution that was unexpected even by Jesus' closest followers was its inclusive nature. Instead of limiting his ministry to Israel and those considered worthy of God's favor, Jesus went out of his way to minister to those shunned by the religious leadership. He healed the servant of a Roman centurion, and commended him for his remarkable faith (Matthew 8:5–13). Luke, who gives more attention to Jesus' ministry to outcasts, records Jesus' encounter with Zacchaeus, a despised tax collector. Because Zacchaeus repented and promised to repay those he had cheated and help the poor, Jesus commended him as a true son of Abraham. The Jesus revolution was for everyone, especially those who were considered ethnic, social, moral outsiders, but who Jesus considered insiders. This emphasis is particularly stressed in Jesus' parables.

The "Already but Not Yet" Kingdom

Because of Jesus' announcement—"the kingdom of God has come near"—most believe that Jesus inaugurated the kingdom. Some believe it was fully inaugurated. The theological terminology is *realized eschatology*. An older dispensational view is that Jesus announced the coming of the kingdom, but because the Jewish leaders officially rejected Jesus, he did not inaugurate the kingdom. This is the "postponed kingdom" view. My view, and the one that I think is most consistent with the scriptural evidence, is that Jesus inaugurated the kingdom, but the complete fulfillment is future. In the Lord's Prayer, Jesus instructed us to pray, "Your kingdom come, your will be done, on earth as it is in heaven" (Matthew 6:10). It seems as if Jesus is encouraging us to pray for the future completion of the kingdom of heaven that has already invaded earth. In his final Passover meal, Jesus assured the Twelve that he would not celebrate the meal "until that day when I drink it new with you in my Father's kingdom" (Matthew 26:29). Again, Jesus anticipates a future aspect of the kingdom.

Theologians refer to this phenomenon as the "already but not yet" kingdom—a prominent feature in many of Jesus' parables.

New Treasures

After Jesus began teaching in parables, he asked his disciples, "'Have you understood all these things?' . . . 'Yes,' they replied" (Matthew 13:51). Jesus informed them that those who understand parables are like scribes. They can teach old truths about the law but also new truths about the kingdom of God. Jesus compares these new truths (mysteries) to a valuable treasure (Matthew 13:52). Though at times difficult, I think we would agree that the kingdom truths Jesus revealed in his parables are like an incomparable treasure.

To enable you (the reader) to unlock the truths hidden in Jesus' parables, I suggest the following guidelines:

1. Context. Relate the parable to the cultural context of first-century Palestine and the historical context of Jesus' ministry. Jesus told stories related to everyday life in Israel. Israel was a Jewish nation but had been significantly influenced by

Greek and Roman culture. In reading a parable, we should first consider what the story meant to Jesus' audience, not to those of us who live in twentieth-century America.

From a historical perspective, we need to remember that Jesus fulfilled Old Testament promises. A kingdom perspective is essential to understanding Jesus' parables. We should ask, "What is the new kingdom truth or truths in the story?" The mysteries of the kingdom are new truths about the nature of the kingdom of God that are different or clarification of what was envisioned in the Old Testament.

2. Purpose. Not always, but often, Jesus stated the purpose either before or after the parable. Jesus was a Master Teacher and had the uncanny ability to seize teachable moments. For example, when he was invited to the home of a prominent Pharisee, Jesus noticed how the other guests were scrambling to get the most prestigious seats. Jesus told a story about a wedding banquet to teach about humility (Luke 14:7–11). There is no preceding context for the parable of the shrewd manager, but Jesus gives the purpose at the end of the story. He says to use your earthly possessions to help others and you will be welcomed into your eternal home (Luke 16:1–9).

We must also remember that Jesus' purpose was not to entertain. Though he told stories with surprising twists and turns to capture and hold people's attention, Jesus' purpose was to challenge and impress on his followers the need to change their mindset about how they related to God and others. In the parable of the wedding banquet, mentioned above, the other guests must have been shocked when Jesus told them to take the least desirable seats, then they would be honored when the host invited them to take the seats of honor (Luke 14:7–11). Sinners probably smiled and the Pharisees undoubtedly grimaced when, in the parables of the lost sheep and the lost coin, Jesus said that heaven celebrates when one sinner repents (Luke 15:1–10).

3. Main point/points. In the early history of the church, parables were often interpreted as allegories, giving meaning to every detail of the parable. The classic example is Augustine's interpretation of the parable of the good Samaritan. His interpretation is as follows: The man who went down from Jerusalem represents Adam and Jerusalem, the heavenly city of peace from which the man fell. The thieves are the devil and his angels. The priest and the Levite are ministers in the Old Testament. The Good Samaritan is God, and the beast is the flesh and refers to Jesus' incarnation. The inn is the church. And so forth. This kind of approach was obviously the imposing of Christian doctrine on the story.

Later in the history of the church, to avoid allegory, interpreters insisted that parables contain only one main point, a view that prevailed until recently. Now interpreters realize that limiting a parable to one main point eliminates the creative richness of Jesus as a storyteller, and it is almost impossible to state the purpose of some parables in a single statement; thus, they recognize that more than one of the details of the story can have meaning. This is the view of New Testament scholar Craig Blomberg and others. Blomberg suggests limiting the main points of the parable to the number of main characters in the story, and categorizes parables as three, two, or one parable.[2] Blomberg's approach is helpful for avoiding turning parables into allegories, and the main principle is that we should give symbolic meaning only to features of the story that are consistent with the progressive advance of God's unfolding plan of redemption and Jewish culture in the time of Jesus. The question to ask: "What would Jesus' audience have understood from the story?" It is unlikely that the Jews, even Jesus' closest followers, would have connected the inn with the church in Augustine's interpretation of the parable of the good Samaritan.

However, by their very nature, parables introduce new and unexpected truths about the inauguration and growth of the kingdom; thus, Jesus' audience would have been surprised by what Jesus intended. And it's obvious that some parables anticipate the future, especially those about the advance of the kingdom and final judgment.

4. Application. Since Jesus intended parables to bring about life change, we must ultimately ask, "So what?" How do I respond? What new truth have I learned about God, myself, and others? How will this change how I think and act? Though application is subjective in that it will be somewhat different for each of us, we need to prayerfully reflect on the story and allow the Holy Spirit to speak to us through the parabolic voice of Jesus. I have found Ezra 7:10 helpful for the study and application of all of Scripture: "For Ezra had devoted himself to the study and observance of the law of the Lord, and to teaching its decrees and laws in Israel."

I hope these studies will help you to become a scribe like Ezra, who can understand, apply, and teach the old and new mysteries of the kingdom from the treasure of Jesus' parables.

The Trees and the Thornbush King

Judges 9:7–21

AUTHOR'S TAKEAWAY: *Be careful of what you ask for—you might get it.*

Some might describe the current moral and spiritual environment in America as "everyone doing what is right in his or her own eyes." This is not the first time in history that people have abandoned any kind of higher moral standard to do whatever they wanted. The era of the judges was similarly characterized, and it was one of the worst eras in Israel's history. Without a godly and charismatic national leader, God's people spiraled downward into a cesspool of spiritual apostasy and tribal warfare. They were repeatedly oppressed by surrounding nations and seduced to adopt their pagan practices. To rescue his people from their enemies, God raised up judges. Unlike judges today, these judges were military and spiritual leaders, not judiciary officials. The judges were flawed, but they were able to slow the descent into chaos. As the plot unfolds in the book of Judges, it becomes increasingly apparent that Israel desperately needed a king.

The parable of the trees is a story told by Jotham to rebuke the people of Shechem for choosing an evil king. It is one of many illustrations in the book of Judges that exposes the disastrous consequences when people abandon God and do whatever seems right to them. Gideon was the fourth of six major judges. God empowered him to rout a superior force of Midianites in a surprise attack in the middle of the night. But unfortunately, after he died, the Israelites rejected Gideon's family, abandoned the Lord, and worshiped the detestable Baals (Judges 8:33–35). Jotham and Abimelech were two of Gideon's seventy-one sons. Abimelech was his son by a concubine from Shechem, so Jotham and Abimelech were only half brothers. Abimelech conspired with the citizens of Shechem to become their king. Perhaps because his half brothers shunned him, he hired hit men to murder all of Gideon's sons. But Jotham escaped. And when the people of Shechem gathered to make the murderous Abimelech their king, Jotham climbed Mount Gerizim across the valley from Shechem, and shouted out the parable of the trees.

The Trees

The Lord of the Rings by J. R. R. Tolkien is a wonderful fantasy about the struggle between good and evil. As the plot unfolds, trees join the fight to save Middle Earth from the evil Sauron. Like the courageous trees in Tolkien's fantasy, the trees in Jotham's fable also have human characteristics.

We don't know if Jotham preplanned his speech or if it was spontaneous, but it was certainly clever and effective. In the story, trees are seeking a king, but the most important and productive trees in Israel refuse to become their king. First, the olive tree declines because it is busy producing olive oil in the service of both the gods and man, and is not interested in ruling over trees that simply wave their branches in the wind—an action (or nonaction) that brings up images of uselessness. Next, the fig tree says the same. It would rather produce sweet fruit than rule as king over useless trees. The trees pleaded with the grapevine to be their king, but the grapevine also refused. "Should I give up my wine, which cheers both gods and humans, to hold sway over the trees?" asked the grapevine.

The Thornbush

In desperation, the trees plead with the thornbush to become their king. The thornbush conditionally agrees. "If you really want to anoint me king over you, come and take refuge in my shade" (Judges 9:15). This is extreme irony because thornbushes are so small they can't provide much shade. The thornbush adds a warning. "But if not, then let fire come out of the thornbush and consume the cedars of Lebanon!" (Judges 9:15). Because thornbushes are extremely dry, they are susceptible to fire that can quickly spread and burn an entire forest.

The Shechemites

Jotham applies the parable directly to the Shechemites. They are dumber than trees, and have made a terrible mistake in anointing Abimelech as their king. He is a thornbush. Jotham reminds them of how his father, Gideon, had risked his life to rescue them from the Midianites, and says that they repaid him with treachery by murdering his seventy other sons and choosing Abimelech as their king. He warns them of reciprocal justice. He wishes them happiness if they acted in good faith; but if their intentions were evil, he predicts severe judgment in the form of a curse. "But if you have not, let fire come out from Abimelech and consume you, the citizens of Shechem and Beth Millo, and let fire come out from you, the citizens of Shechem and Beth Millo, and consume Abimelek!" (Judges 9:20).

Knowing that his half brother is violent and dangerous, Jotham flees to Beer, an unknown location.

19

|||||||||||||||||||||||||||||||||||| **REFLECT** ||||||||||||||||||||||||||||||||||||

1. Read Genesis 6:9. What are some of the ways that Noah's lifestyle is a contrast to the lifestyle of people during the time of the judges, when everyone did what was right in his or her own eyes? How do you nurture and maintain a lifestyle that is pleasing to God?

2. Read Judges 9:9–13. Why do you think the olive tree, the fig tree, and the vine refused to become king of the Shechemites? What are some of the reasons you would not become the leader of an organization?

3. What three principles would you use for selecting leaders in a church, civic organization, or political office?

4. Read Judges 9:16–20. Jotham stated that the actions of the Shechemites would merit either divine blessings or judgment.

   a. What does Jotham's statement imply about the justice of God?

   b. What does it imply about the consequences of our choices?

5. We all make mistakes. What is one mistake that you have made, and what were the consequences? What could you have done differently to avoid the mistake? What life lesson or lessons did you learn from the experience?

6. How could you use this story to explain to high-schoolers that choices in life have consequences?

|||||||||||||||||||||||||||||||||||| **OPTIONAL** ||||||||||||||||||||||||||||||||||||

1. Read Judges 9:22–57 for the consequences of the Shechemites' choice of Abimelech and the fulfillment of Jotham's curse.

a. See Judges 9:22–25. How did God act to fulfill Jotham's curse? In the NLT, verse 23 reads, "God sent a spirit that stirred up trouble between Abimelech and the leading citizens of Shechem, and they revolted." What does this verse suggest about God's sovereign control over spirits, both good and evil?

b. What happened to the citizens of Shechem?

c. What happened to Abimelech?

d. How is Judges 9 a vivid illustration of the descriptive phrase, "Everyone did what was right in his or her own eyes"?

2. See Judges 21:25. How is the current era in America like the era of the Judges?

|||||||||||||||||||||||||||||| **Memory Verse** ||||||||||||||||||||||||||||||

This is the account of Noah and his family. Noah was a righteous man, blameless among the people of his time, and he walked faithfully with God.

Genesis 6:9

The Rich Man
and the Poor Man

2 Samuel 12:1–12

AUTHOR'S TAKEAWAY: *If I had only known . . .*

All of us have had "If I had only known" moments. One of mine was when I was seven. My friends and I were playing outside when we noticed an elderly lady sitting in her backyard enjoying the sun. We conspired to frighten her, and hid behind an old trailer. My friends crawled under it and gave me the general direction to throw a rock, which was supposed to land near her but not hit her. Yep, you guessed it. It hit her. My friends shot out from under the trailer and said, "You hit her in the head!" We all ran home. I thought I was safe because no one was home, but after what seemed like an eternity, I heard a knock on the door. I kept stone-quiet, hoping they would think no one was home. But they knocked again and again, and then I heard a loud voice: "This is the police. Open the door." My heart sank. I was only seven years old, and I was going to prison for murder. That obviously didn't happen; the rock, fortunately, hit her in the shoulder, not the head. But I have never forgotten that experience. "If I had only known . . ."

Nathan, a prophet during the united kingdom era, used a parable about a rich man and a poor man to rebuke David for his sin with Bathsheba. Instead of leading his army in the spring campaign against the Ammonites, David stayed behind in Jerusalem. He was not necessarily negligent because he was confident Joab could effectively command the army. In the early afternoon, David saw a beautiful woman bathing on the roof of her house. Bathsheba apparently did not think anyone would see her from the roof of the palace, but David did. He summoned her to the palace, and she complied. We don't know if she was compelled to go to the palace or went voluntarily, but regardless, she shouldn't have gone. David slept with her and thought no one would know he had violated another man's wife. But he was wrong.

When Bathsheba told David she was pregnant, he immediately tried to hide his sin. David summoned Bathsheba's husband, Uriah, to Jerusalem, and encouraged him to go home. But Uriah was a devoted soldier and refused to enjoy the comfort of his home and wife while his fellow soldiers were enduring the hardships of a military campaign. David then sent Uriah back to the army with secret instructions for Joab to put Uriah dangerously close to the wall, where he would probably be killed. Joab did as David commanded, and informed the king that Uriah had been killed.

In historical narrative, writers almost never make comments about whether the action of the characters is right or wrong, but David's sin was so offensive that this writer steps out of his role as historian and gives the divine perspective on what had happened: "But the thing David had done displeased the LORD" (2 Samuel 11:27).

A Rich Man and a Poor Man

The Lord sent Nathan to David; but instead of directly rebuking David, Nathan told him a story about a rich man and a poor man. The rich man had a huge flock of sheep and a large herd of cattle.

23

The poor man had only one lamb that he cherished and treated like one of his family. When a guest arrived at the home of the rich man, instead of killing one of his own sheep to feed his guest, he forcibly took the lamb of the poor man and killed it for his guest.

David was incensed and demanded that the rich man repay the poor man four times what he had stolen from him.

Nathan and David

Though the identity of the two men in the story should have been rather obvious, Nathan pointed at David and said, "You are the man!" (2 Samuel 12:7). As God's prophetic spokesman, Nathan then announced judgment on David. He reminded David of how greatly the Lord had blessed him. He had protected David from Saul's murderous attempts to kill him, gave him Saul's possessions including his wives, made him king over Israel and Judah, and would have done even more for him.

In return, David had despised the Lord by doing evil. He had Uriah murdered and stole his wife. God is kind and forgiving, but there are inevitable consequences for sin. Nathan said that because of his high crimes, his kingdom would never enjoy peace. David had sinned secretly, but his retribution would be public: One of David's own family would violate his wives in the sight of all Israel.

David's response is remarkable. He confessed, "I have sinned against the LORD" (2 Samuel 12:13). David had sinned against Bathsheba. He had sinned against Uriah, Joab and the army, and all Israel. Yet he correctly recognized that his greatest offense was against the Lord. David's humility in owning his sin is one of the primary reasons that he became the ideal model for the kings of Judah and Israel. For example, in the divine critique of Abijah's rule, the writer says, "He committed all the sins his father had done before him; his heart was not fully devoted to the LORD his God, as the heart of David his forefather had been" (1 Kings 15:3). David was obviously not perfect, but unlike most of the kings after him, he was willing to humble himself and seek forgiveness when he sinned. His full confession is in Psalm 51.

David's sin was a capital offense, but the Lord was merciful. Nathan said, "The LORD has taken away your sin. You are not going to die" (2 Samuel 12:13). Because David had despised the Lord, he would suffer the painful consequences of his sin. Nathan predicted, "The son born to you will die" (2 Samuel 12:14). To reemphasize David's violation of another man's wife, Nathan refers to Bathsheba as Uriah's wife: "The LORD struck the child that Uriah's wife had borne to David, and he became ill" (2 Samuel 12:15). Though David fasted and prayed, the child died. After the child's death, David's response surprised his servants. Instead of mourning as was customary, David washed, put on clean clothes, worshiped, and ate a meal. When asked why he didn't mourn, David told his servants that while the child was living, there was hope that the Lord would spare him; but once he had died, he could not be brought back to life. Instead of the dead returning to the living, David realized that the living would go to the dead.

REFLECT

1. Read 1 Corinthians 6:18. What do you think David and Bathsheba could (should) have done differently to avoid putting themselves in a compromising situation? Are there any changes you need to make in your lifestyle to avoid temptation?

2. Read 2 Samuel 11:27. Why do you think the author gives a divine commentary on David's sin? (Remember this is highly unusual in historical narrative.) What does this comment reveal about the nature of David's sin and God's character?

3. Read 2 Samuel 12:1. (See also 1 Thessalonians 2:13; 2 Timothy 3:15–16; 1 Corinthians 6:19–20; and Ephesians

4:30.) The Lord sent Nathan, the prophet, to rebuke David. How does God convict (rebuke) us of sin today?

4. Why do you think Nathan used a parable to confront David rather than directly rebuking him? Do you think this is an effective way to deal with someone who has sinned? Why or why not?

5. Read 2 Samuel 12:22–23. What do these verses imply about the living and the dead? What do they suggest about life after death (the afterlife)?

6. What new truths have you learned from this study about sin and its consequences?

OPTIONAL

1. Read Psalm 51. After approximately one year of refusing to acknowledge his sin, David pleads for forgiveness.
    a. Vv. 1–2: What two aspects of God's character are the basis for David's appeal?
    b. Vv. 3–6: What different words (terms) does David use to describe his sin?
    c. Vv. 7–12: What are four of David's requests?
    d. Vv. 13–17: What does God desire more than sacrifice?

2. Read Psalm 32. This is a companion to Psalm 51. David expresses his gratefulness for God's mercy and forgiveness, what he learned from his experience, and his encouragement to others.
    a. Why does David praise the Lord?
    b. What was David's physical and emotional state before he confessed his sin? What does this reveal about the consequences of sin?
    c. What does David want others to learn from his experience?
    d. What new truth have you learned?

‖‖‖‖‖‖‖‖‖‖‖‖‖‖‖‖‖‖‖‖‖‖‖ **Memory Verse** ‖‖‖‖‖‖‖‖‖‖‖‖‖‖‖‖‖‖‖‖‖‖‖‖‖‖‖

Do not love the world or anything in the world. If anyone loves the world, love for the Father is not in them. For everything in the world—the lust of the flesh, the lust of the eyes, and the pride of life—comes not from the Father but from the world. The world and its desires pass away, but whoever does the will of God lives forever.

1 John 2:15–17

The Nature
of the
Kingdom

The Coming
of the Kingdom

The Sower
and the Soils

Matthew 13:1–23; Mark 4:1–20; Luke 8:1–15

AUTHOR'S TAKEAWAY: *It's the soil.*

The parable of the sower is the first of Jesus' parables, and is recorded in all three of the Synoptic Gospels (Matthew, Mark, and Luke). The crowds following Jesus had grown so large that he climbed into a boat to teach them. He told a story of what happened when a farmer scattered seed in his field. In an agricultural society like first-century Israel, everyone would have easily understood and identified with the sower. From a bag he carried, the sower scattered seed in his field. Some fell on the hard, packed path surrounding his field and was eaten by the birds. Some fell on rocky soil—the patches of limestone that were covered with a thin layer of topsoil. The seed started to grow but quickly wilted in the blazing hot sun because it had no root. Some fell among the weeds. The farmer had tried to rid his field of weeds, but like dandelions in a lawn, he couldn't get them all. They grew and choked the plants. All of this sounds discouraging, but these are the kinds of problems that made farming so difficult.

The Parable of the Sower and the six other parables recorded in Matthew 13 are listed in the following chart, as well as an eighth that is recorded only in the Gospel of Mark.

Parables	Meaning	Kingdom Truth
The Sower	The competing obstacles to the proclamation of the Word of God	The remarkable growth of the kingdom of God in spite of competing obstacles
The Secret Growth of the Seed (see also Mark 4:26–29)	The mysterious (secret) growth of the kingdom in the present age	The sovereign power of God in establishing the kingdom in all its fullness
The Wheat and Weeds	The coexistence of believers and unbelievers in the present age	The separation of the righteous from the unrighteous in the day of judgment
The Mustard Seed	The amazing growth of the kingdom from a small beginning	Though small in the beginning, the kingdom will become universal and inclusive of all nations
The Leaven (Yeast)	The pervasive and powerful growth of the kingdom	The kingdom expands powerfully and is impossible to stop
The Hidden Treasure and the Pearl of Great Price	The selling of everything to buy a hidden treasure and perfect pearl	The incomparable value of the kingdom
The Fishing Net	Separation of believers from unbelievers	Blessing of the righteous and judgment of the unrighteous at the end of the present age

A Surprising Harvest

Jesus' stories always include a surprising twist, and that's the good news in this parable. A quarter of the seed fell on good soil, and the harvest was incredible. The seed produced a crop of a hundred, sixty, or thirty times what was planted. The harvest was far above what farmers could expect—in first-century Israel, most farmers would have been satisfied with a yield of ten percent.

Insiders and Outsiders

Because Jesus hadn't previously taught in parables, his disciples didn't understand. They asked, "Why do you speak to the people in parables?" (Matthew 13:10). Jesus' answer is important for understanding both the practical and theological purpose of parables.

In both Matthew and Mark, Jesus makes a distinction between "insiders" and "outsiders." "He replied, 'Because the knowledge of the secrets of the kingdom of heaven has been given to you, but not to them'" (Matthew 13:11; see also Mark 4:11). Jesus' answer raises two questions. One, what did Jesus mean by "the secrets [literally *mysteries*] of the kingdom of heaven"? Two, did Jesus use parables to hide truths about the kingdom from some but not others, which would seem counterproductive to his kingdom mission?

Mysteries

When we hear the word *mystery*, we typically think of an unexplained happening or a crime like *Murder on the Orient Express*. In Scripture, *mystery* (*mysterion*) refers to truths about the kingdom of God that have been hidden in the past but are now revealed. The seven parables in Matthew 13 reveal truths about the kingdom that were not previously known and could not have been known if God had not revealed them.

Matthew places the parables after opposition from the religious leaders. In Matthew 12:24, when Jesus healed a man who was demon-possessed and suffering multiple handicaps, instead of recognizing the miracle as evidence of the kingdom, the Pharisees accused him of using the power of Satan (Beelzebul). After warning them of the terrible consequences of deliberate and persistent unbelief, Jesus began teaching in parables. His parables both revealed and concealed truths about the kingdom. Those with good hearts understood Jesus' parables. Those with hard and stubborn hearts didn't. From a practical perspective, Jesus' teaching resulted in a division between insiders and outsiders. In Mark, the quote from Isaiah is forceful and suggests a theological reason why outsiders cannot understand parables (Mark 4:11–12). Because they have hardened their hearts, God has hardened their hearts. They cannot understand and repent and be forgiven because they are under divine judgment—a prerogative that only God can impose on persistent and intentional unbelief.

Mark also includes Jesus' rebuke of his disciples, "Don't you understand this parable? How then will you understand any parable?" (Mark 4:13). Though Jesus' closest followers (insiders) should have understood, they didn't, so Jesus explained the parable to them. The parable of the sower, then, is crucial for understanding all parables. What is needed is a "good heart," a desire, and a willingness to accept Jesus' teaching.

Bad and Good Soil

The sower (farmer) is not identified in the parable. The emphasis is on the seed and where it falls. Jesus identifies four kinds of soil. The seed falls on hard, rocky, thorny, and good soil. In the explanation, Jesus identifies the seed as the Word of God. The four kinds of soil represent four different responses of people to the Word of God—in the Gospels, the proclamation of the Good News about the kingdom.

Hard Soil—The seed that fell on the path could not grow because the ground was too hard. The birds ate the seed before it could germinate. In Mark, Jesus explained that the birds represent Satan. Matthew identifies the birds as "the evil one," and Luke identifies them as "the devil." Though the devil was introduced as an adversary of Jesus when he was tempted, this is the first time he is revealed as an enemy of the kingdom. Jesus will reveal more about the devil's opposition to the kingdom in the parable of the weeds.

Rocky Soil—The seed that falls on rocky soil grows quickly, but it also wilts quickly under the hot sun. The rocky soil represents people who make a superficial response to the gospel without counting the cost. They receive the message with joy but quickly abandon their faith because of trouble or persecution.

Thorny Soil—The seed sown among the thorns actually grows, but so do the weeds. And unfortunately, the weeds grow more profusely, depriving the seed of moisture and nutrients, choking it out. The thorny soil represents those who abandon their faith because of worldly worries and the lure of wealth. These are people with a divided heart. For them, following Christ is not either/or but both/and. Jesus will warn about the impossibility of serving God and money (Luke 16:13), and in his teaching on the cost of discipleship, he will demand a total commitment: "Those of you who do not give up everything you have cannot be my disciples" (Luke 14:33).

Good Soil—If you were listening to Jesus tell the story of the sower, you would have been surprised by the ending. Some seed falls on good soil and produces a remarkable harvest. Matthew says it was thirty, sixty, and even a hundred times what was sown. Luke simply says it produces a hundred times what was sown (Luke 8:8). Though some believe these numbers represent varying degrees of works by Jesus' followers, that interpretation misses the point. Jesus' point is to assure his followers of the growth of the kingdom through the proclamation of the Word. The various degrees of the harvest are to emphasize the abundance of the harvest. Though Jesus does not identify the sower, in the parable of the weeds, Jesus refers to himself as the sower, "The one who sowed the good seed is the Son of Man" (Matthew 13:37). However, in correcting the personality cult in the church at Corinth, Paul says that he and Apollos are only servants (sowers), whereas "God makes the seed grow" (1 Corinthians 3:7 NLT). So both Christ and then his followers are "sowers" of the Word.

The Power of the Gospel

What is often missed in the interpretation is Jesus' stated purpose for teaching in parables. Jesus said that he used parables to

35

reveal secrets (new truths) about the nature of the kingdom, so we need to ask, What is the new truth about the kingdom? Based on the kingdom promised in the Old Testament, the Jews expected universal acceptance of the kingdom by the people of God and the total destruction of their enemies. Opposition to Jesus from Israel's leadership was undoubtedly surprising and discouraging to his disciples. In the context of Matthew, Jesus' teaching new truths about the kingdom follows the sinister plot by the religious leaders to destroy him and the diabolical accusation that his power over demons was from Satan (Matthew 12:1–15, 24). So to hide kingdom truths from his enemies and to reveal them to his disciples, Jesus began teaching in parables.

What then is the new kingdom truth for the disciples and for us? It is the assurance that through the proclamation of the Word, we will advance the kingdom, though for various reasons, some (perhaps most) will not respond. It is important to note the growth of the kingdom does not depend upon the sower but on the seed (the Word). This is a truth stated in Paul's prayer for the Colossians, "In the same way, the gospel is bearing fruit and growing throughout the whole world" (Colossians 1:6).

|||||||||||||||||||||||||||||||||||||| **REFLECT** ||||||||||||||||||||||||||||||||||||||

1. Why do you think the emphasis in the parable is on the seed and not the farmer (sower) or the planting and harvesting process? See 1 Corinthians 3:5–9; Colossians 1:3–8.

2. How would you encourage a high school student whose friend became angry when they shared the gospel with them?

3. How would you describe a person with a hard heart?

4. What are some of the ways that Satan keeps the Word from penetrating into the hearts of hearers?

5. What are some of the competing desires (weeds) in sharing the gospel with people in America? What can we do to
   overcome deceitful attractions of the world?

6. Read Mark 4:15; Luke 8:3; and Psalm 1:3. What are the
   differences between a person who makes a superficial response (rocky soil) to the gospel and a righteous person
   described as a tree planted by streams of water?

7. How does this parable give you confidence to share the
   gospel?

8. Why do you think the sower cast seed everywhere instead
   of sowing more on the good soil and less on the soil he
   knew wouldn't produce a harvest? What is the implication for the proclamation of the gospel? Can we know the
   hearts of those who hear the good news?

9. Read James 1:22–25. Though this parable is primarily
   about unbelievers and their response to the Word, how
   are we sometimes closed-minded, superficial, or distracted
   when we hear the Word of God? How does James urge us
   to respond?

10. How would you describe your heart right now?

IIIIIIIIIIIIIIIIIIIIIIIIIIIIIIII **Memory Verse** IIIIIIIIIIIIIIIIIIIIIIIIIIIIIIII

For I am not ashamed of this Good News about Christ. It is the
power of God at work, saving everyone who believes—the Jew first
and also the Gentile. This Good News tells us how God makes
us right in his sight. This is accomplished from start to finish by
faith. As the Scriptures say, "It is through faith that a righteous
person has life."

Romans 1:16–17 NLT

The Wheat
and Weeds

Matthew 13:24–29, 36–43

AUTHOR'S TAKEAWAY: *Sometimes it's difficult
to tell the difference between
the good and the bad.*

Weeds are insidious little monsters. My wife is the gardener in our family. She does the planting, watering, cultivating, and fertilizing. My job is to do the weeding. When weeds first start growing, they look like the good plants. If you try to pull them out, you will pull out the good plants along with the weeds. But if you wait too long, the roots of the weeds become intertwined with the roots of the good plants, and then you can't pull out the weeds without uprooting the good plants.

Jesus told a story about weeds in a field of wheat. It is the second of seven parables recorded in Matthew 13, and it is found only in Matthew. Though the parable is about the planting of "good seed," the focus is mainly on the attempt by an enemy to destroy the wheat by secretly sowing weeds among the good seed.

Though Jesus spoke the parable publicly, he explained it privately only to his disciples.

Wheat and Weeds

As he did in the parable of the sower, Jesus uses sowing and harvesting to teach about the kingdom of heaven.

A farmer planted good seed (seed that was weed free) in his field. We are not given any details about the sowing; instead, Jesus inserts a villain in the story. While everyone was sleeping, an enemy scattered bad seed in the same field. The bad seed was darnel (NASB), which is difficult to distinguish from wheat but is toxic. Jesus does not identify the enemy or give the reason he tried to destroy the farmer's crop. Throughout the Middle East, people who had been offended would sometimes try to get even by secretly sowing darnel in the field of the person who had offended them.

When the plants sprouted, the farmer's servants realized that something terrible had happened; weeds were growing with the wheat. They asked, "Where did the weeds come from?" The farmer knew. He had been careful to plant only good seed. He told his servants, "An enemy did this." The servants wanted to pull out the weeds immediately, but the wise farmer said no. He knew they couldn't pull out the weeds without destroying the wheat, and they could separate the darnel from the wheat at harvest time. At harvest, the workers could more easily identify the darnel, tie it in bundles, and burn it. They could also bundle the wheat and bring it into the barn.

Secrets of the Kingdom

Without Jesus' explanation, it would be impossible to know the precise kingdom application. So later, when he was alone with his disciples, Jesus explained the parable (13:31–34).

He identified the following:

The Kingdom Revolution

Sower	Son of Man (Jesus)
Field	World
Good seed	People of the kingdom
Bad seed	People of the evil one
Enemy	Devil
Harvest	End of the age (separation and judgment of the wicked and reward the righteous)
Harvesters	Angels

The parable reveals several new truths about the revolution inaugurated by Jesus.

1. The Jews expected the Lord to immediately destroy the wicked and deliver the righteous when he came to fulfill his kingdom promises, so Jesus' teaching that both good and evil will coexist until the end of the present age was revolutionary. At the consummation—not the inauguration—of the kingdom, God will send his angels to separate the righteous from the unrighteous. The righteous will be blessed; the unrighteous judged.

2. To encourage his disciples, who were becoming increasingly worried about opposition, Jesus revealed that they would face hostility to the end of the age; and it was not possible to separate the good from the evil.

3. Though Jesus' confrontation with Satan in the wilderness was a foreshadowing of his ultimate victory, the devil remains a force of evil in the world. The word *devil* means "slanderer" and is a common designation for Satan in the New Testament. Because Jesus sought to establish his kingdom in the world, it was inevitable that he would be opposed by Satan. The devil is the enemy of the Son of Man and the messianic kingdom, and continues to sow evil in the present age.

4. The field is the world, not a cryptic reference to the church. Jesus is the Son of Man, who is destined to rule over the world (see Daniel 7:13–14).

################################ **REFLECT** ################################

1. Read Matthew 13:37–39. Why is there so much evil in the world if Jesus inaugurated the kingdom?
2. Read Matthew 7:1. How is the parable of the wheat and weeds a commentary on Matthew 7:1?
3. Read Matthew 13:28–30. Why does Jesus teach that we must leave the ultimate judgment of good and evil to God? What are the dangers of judging other people (see Matthew 7:1)?
4. Read Matthew 13:37–39.

   a. Why are people reluctant or unwilling to recognize evil in the world as the work of Satan?

   b. What are some of the strategies Satan uses to sow evil in the world?
5. Though the parable is about the kingdom of heaven, it can be applied to individual Christians.

   a. Ephesians 6:10–17; James 4:7. If we think of our relationship with Christ as a garden, how can we prevent the devil from sowing weeds in our garden?

   b. Ephesians 4:20–26; Colossians 3:1–16. Though the parable teaches we should not judge others, it does not prohibit us from judging ourselves. What does Paul exhort us to do about weeds in our lives?
6. Read Matthew 13:40–43.

   a. What does this parable teach about the ultimate fate of the righteous and the wicked?

   b. Why do you think God is waiting until the end of the age to separate the wicked from the righteous?

7. How is the danger of a computer virus like the parable of the wheat and weeds? What analogies would you make between a computer virus and the parable of the wheat and weeds?

|||||||||||||||||||||||||||||||||| **OPTIONAL** ||||||||||||||||||||||||||||||||||

1. Read Daniel 7:13–14. Why does Jesus use the title "son of man" in the parable rather than a different messianic title?

|||||||||||||||||||||||||||||||||| **Memory Verse** ||||||||||||||||||||||||||||||||||

But the fruit of the Spirit is love, joy, peace, forbearance, kindness, goodness, faithfulness, gentleness and self-control. Against such things there is no law.

Galatians 5:22–23

The Seed
Growing Secretly

Mark 4:26–29

AUTHOR'S TAKEAWAY: *Sometimes what is not seen is more important than what is seen.*

My wife's father and his five brothers grew potatoes and wheat in the Red River Valley in North Dakota. I don't know much about farming, but I know farmers work hard and are somewhat dependent on Mother Nature, who is very unpredictable. When I began studying the parable of the seed growing secretly, I thought of the amazing patience and faith of my father-in-law and his brothers. They plant the seed and wait. And if it rains, but not too much, you will soon see little green plants push their way up through the rich black soil of the Red River Valley. They can't see what's going on below the topsoil, but they are confident the potatoes are growing. What happens in the farmland of North Dakota is the phenomenon behind the story of the secret but certain growth of the seed.

The parable of the seed growing secretly is recorded in Mark 4, along with two other seed parables and the parable of the lamp.

Jesus identifies it as a kingdom parable: "This is what the kingdom of God is like" (Mark 4:26). Because of the opposition, Jesus told the story to reassure his disciples that though there was not a spectacular manifestation of the coming of the kingdom, the kingdom was secretly growing.

The Farmer Doesn't Know How

As in the parable of the sower, a farmer scatters seed; but instead of identifying different kinds of soil, Jesus describes the different stages of growth. The farmer doesn't know how, but the seed sprouts and grows by itself in three successive stages. First, a leaf pushes its way up through the soil, then a head of grain is formed, and finally the wheat ripens. How it grows is a mystery, but growth is certain. When the grain is ripe, it is time for the farmer to harvest.

Commentators have interpreted the parable in three different ways. Some think the parable is about evangelism, others believe it is about different stages of spiritual growth in the life of a believer, and still others believe it is about the inevitable growth of the kingdom under the sovereign power of God.[1] Like the parable of the sower, the key to interpreting the parable is to recognize that it is about the kingdom.

God's Power and the Growth of the Kingdom

The parable emphasizes the sovereign power of God in establishing his kingdom. The growth is mysterious (invisible) but certain. And though the kingdom was only partially inaugurated at Jesus' first coming, it will be fully manifested at his second coming. It has been suggested that the invisible growth of the seed is a veiled reference to the Holy Spirit, but this seems unlikely since Jesus had not yet taught about the ministry of the Spirit in the preaching of the gospel.

The farmer represents God and, by extension, he also represents Jesus and his followers. We, as believers, are responsible for advancing the kingdom by the proclamation of the gospel (Word), but the growth depends upon God's power, not ours.

IIIIIIIIIIIIIIIIIIIIIIIIIIIIIIIIIIIIIIII **REFLECT** IIIIIIIIIIIIIIIIIIIIIIIIIIIIIIIIIIIIIIII

1. What is the surprising twist in this parable? What did the farmer do after he had sowed the seed? Why do you think Jesus did not tell a story encouraging more active participation in establishing the kingdom?

2. What is the primary means for the growth of the kingdom? What is the fruit of the gospel according to Colossians 1:7? If available, check the *NLT Study Bible*. How has your life been changed by the gospel?

3. How does this parable emphasize that the growth of the kingdom is entirely by God's sovereign power and not human effort? How does this parable encourage you in serving Christ?

4. Instead of leading an open revolt against the Romans, how does this parable describe Jesus' ministry in inaugurating the kingdom?

5. Read James 5:7 and 2 Peter 3:9.
   a. How does this parable encourage patience in serving Christ, especially in proclaiming the Good News?
   b. Why is the Lord patient before judging (harvesting) the earth?

6. Why is it unlikely, as some have suggested, that this parable refers to the invisible working of the Holy Spirit? What is one aspect of the Spirit's ministry in planting the seed (proclaiming the Word), according to 1 Thessalonians 1:4–7?

7. Read 1 Corinthians 3:5–9. How does Paul's description of the ministry support the main truth of this parable?

8. Read Joel 3:11–16 and Revelation 14:14–20.

  a. What does the harvest represent in the parable?

  b. What will happen to the enemies of the people of God? What will happen to God's people?

  c. What is the common theme in Joel, this parable, and Revelation? Though these passages were written by different authors hundreds of years apart, what do they reveal about the unity of Scripture? About inspiration?

9 One theological viewpoint about the future is that the world will progressively get better and better until the kingdom is fully realized, and then Christ will return as king (postmillennialism, after the millennial kingdom). How is the ending of this parable an argument against the view that the kingdom will grow until it encompasses the whole earth?

10. Read Matthew 24:14 and Revelation 7:9–10. When will the task of evangelism (sowing and harvesting) be completed? What can you do to encourage a kingdom view that includes a proactive effort to proclaim the Good News to all nations?

||||||||||||||||||||||||||||||| **Memory Verse** |||||||||||||||||||||||||||||||||||

The faith and love that spring from the hope stored up for you in heaven and about which you have already heard in the true message of the gospel that has come to you. In the same way, the gospel is bearing fruit and grows throughout the whole world—just as it has been doing among you since the day you heard it and truly understood God's grace.

Colossians 1:5–6

The Leaven

Matthew 13:33; Luke 13:20–21

AUTHOR'S TAKEAWAY: *Why not make pancakes for your kids?*

When our children were young, it was a tradition for me to make pancakes or waffles on Saturdays. I made them from scratch with whole-wheat flour, buttermilk, baking soda, etc., and I made all kinds—pecan waffles, blueberry pancakes, and the kids' favorite, strawberry waffles with whipped cream. I never measured anything, which bothered people who wanted the recipe. I was well-known in the family for my pancakes and waffles, so I was not surprised when my wife's aunt gave me a sourdough starter kit. Though I liked sourdough pancakes, they were not a favorite of the kids. After the first batch, I kept a small amount of the sourdough for the next batch of pancakes.

People in the first century would have readily understood the parable of the leaven and the process of using yeast to make bread. That is how women, especially the poor, made bread in the first century. They would mix a small amount of fermented yeast with the dough and allow the leaven to work its way through the whole batch. Then they would save a small amount for the next time they made bread.

Small but Powerful

The parable of the leaven is paired with the parable of the mustard seed in Matthew and Luke (Matthew 13:33; Luke 13:20–21), but is omitted in Mark, probably because Mark intentionally gives a shorter and more focused account on Jesus' deeds rather than his teaching.

Because leaven or yeast usually symbolizes evil, some believe it is a symbol for evil in the era between the inauguration of the kingdom and its culmination. The children of Israel were commanded to bake unleavened bread in preparation for the Passover (Exodus 12:8). Jesus compared the lifestyle of the Pharisees to leaven, and warned about the permeating influence of their phony piety (Luke 12:1). Paul commanded the Corinthians to expel one of its members because his sexual immorality, like leaven, could potentially corrupt the entire church (1 Corinthians 5:6–8). This view, however, is inconsistent with Jesus' statement about the positive effect of the yeast. Jesus uses it to describe the hidden but powerful, permeating influence of the kingdom (Matthew 13:33).

The leaven, not the woman, is the important element in the parable, though it is noteworthy that Jesus pairs a woman with a man in the parables of the leaven and the mustard seed. Unlike many in the first century, Jesus regarded women and men of equal value. Like the farmer who planted the mustard seed, her role is to add the yeast to the dough. This suggests the kingdom is completely a work of God. Men and women can enter into the kingdom, they can proclaim the Good News of the kingdom, but the establishing of the kingdom is the sovereign work of God.

Though some have suggested the power of the yeast is a cryptic reference to the work of the Spirit, it is unlikely that at this point in Jesus' ministry, anyone would have connected the leaven to the promised Holy Spirit.

The Power of the Kingdom

What is the new revelation (mystery) of the kingdom? Instead of God immediately and powerfully saving his people from their enemies and ruling over the nations, he is bringing in his kingdom slowly but surely through his Son, Jesus. His ministry is the beginning, not the climactic culmination, of God's eternal kingdom of righteousness and peace. Though inaugurated in a hostile and evil world, the world cannot stop the advance of the kingdom. Like yeast that works its way through the whole batch of dough, the advance of the kingdom is certain, powerful, and universal.

REFLECT

Kingdom Truths

1. What similar and different aspects of the kingdom are revealed in the parables of the mustard seed and the leaven?

2. What is some of the evidence that God's kingdom is working its way through the world like leaven?

3. Some believe that the parable of the leaven teaches that the world will get progressively better. Do you agree or disagree with this view? Why or why not?

4. Read 1 Corinthians 15:51–52; Romans 8:18–21; and 2 Thessalonians 1:5–10. When does Paul teach that evil will be destroyed and God's righteous kingdom fully realized?

5. Read Matthew 28:17–20; Acts 1:8; and 1 Peter 2:9–10. Though the church is not the kingdom, how do believers advance the kingdom in the world?

Personal Application

6. Read 2 Corinthians 5:17. How has your faith (union with Christ) worked like leaven through your life? What

attitudes and thoughts have been transformed? What practices have changed? What areas of your life still need to be renewed?

7. Read Matthew 5:13–16. Instead of *leaven*, Jesus uses the metaphors of *salt* and *light* to challenge Christians to influence the world. How can you advance the kingdom in your community and the world?

8. Read Acts 8:1–4. How were the early Christians like leaven?

9. How does this parable motivate you in your personal growth and service for Christ?

||||||||||||||||||||||||||||||| **Memory Verse** |||||||||||||||||||||||||||||||

In the same way, the gospel is bearing fruit and growing throughout the whole world—just as it has been doing among you since the day you heard it and truly understood God's grace.

Colossians 1:6

The Mustard Seed

Matthew 13:31–32; Mark 4:30–33; Luke 13:18–19

AUTHOR'S TAKEAWAY: *It's better to start small and get big than to start big and get small.*

After seminary, I began my ministry as a pastor. I had the opportunity and challenge of starting a new church. The beginning was obviously small, and growth was slow. In talking with an older and more experienced pastor, I admitted I was a bit discouraged. He encouraged me with a truth that I have never forgotten. He said that it is better to start small and grow big than to start big and become small. Jesus captures that truth in the parable of the mustard seed. The parable is recorded in Matthew, Mark, and Luke. The meaning is basically the same in all three gospels, but the emphasis is different in Luke.

The Smallest of Seeds

Matthew and Mark—The mustard seed isn't actually the smallest seed, but in first-century Israel, it was proverbial for anything that had a small beginning and then grew large. The main point in the parable in Matthew and Mark is not about the sower or the soils; it's about the remarkable growth of the plant. Though small, the mustard seed produces an incredibly large plant, growing in a few weeks up to twelve to fifteen feet in height.

The parable was intended for Jesus' disciples, who were discouraged and confused. They believed that Jesus was the promised Messiah, and had hoped that the kingdom revolution had begun. But instead, Jesus had encountered stiff and growing opposition from Israel's religious leaders. In his Gospel, Matthew places Jesus' teaching in parables on the same day the religious leaders charged that Jesus was an agent of Satan (Beelzebul) after he had healed a demon-possessed man (Matthew 12:24). This obviously was not the kind of reception the disciples expected, and they were worried about what would happen to them and Jesus. Instead of a disastrous end, Jesus assured his disciples that though small in the beginning, the kingdom was powerful and would become massive in size.

Luke—Luke's focus is more on the birds that perched in the branches of the mustard tree. He doesn't mention the smallness of the mustard seed, but records only that the kingdom of God is "like a mustard seed, which a man took and planted in his garden. It grew and became a tree, and the birds perched in its branches" (Luke 13:18–19). Luke, the only Gentile writer of the New Testament, emphasizes the inclusion of everyone in the kingdom—women, the poor, the shunned, and the ethnically despised (see Luke 4:16–19). Because of Luke's emphasis on Jesus' ministry to everyone, it is probable that the reference to "the birds" anticipates the inclusion of all nations in the kingdom, especially Gentiles.

Jesus and the Prophets

The contrast between the kingdom imagery of the prophets and Jesus is striking. Ezekiel compares the kingdom to a mighty cedar: "On the mountain heights of Israel I will plant it; it will produce branches and bear fruit and become a splendid cedar. Birds of every kind will nest in it; they will find shelter in the shade of its branches" (Ezekiel 17:23; see also Ezekiel 31:1–9; Daniel 4:9–12). Though his imagery is different, Isaiah anticipates a massive and powerful kingdom. He writes, "In the last days, the mountain of the LORD's temple will be established as the highest of the mountains; it will be exalted above the hills, and all nations will stream to it" (Isaiah 2:2; see also Micah 4:1). Based on references like these, the Jews expected a dramatic revolution with the coming of the kingdom. But Jesus reveals a different kind of growth. And to assure his disciples that they should not be alarmed by a small beginning, Jesus told the parable of the mustard seed. A small beginning was not failure but rather the beginning of a kingdom that would become massive in size and inclusive of all nations.

REFLECT

Kingdom Truths

1. Read Mark 4:30. What questions did Jesus ask to introduce the parable? Why are questions an effective teaching technique?

2. Read Matthew 13:31–32. What did you already know about the kingdom of heaven (God)? What did you learn? How did this parable change your understanding of the kingdom of God?

3. Read Acts 1:15; 2:41; 4:4; 5:14; 6:1, 7; 8:12; 9:31; 11:19. What was the size of the church in the beginning of Acts, and how rapidly did the church grow? Acts ends with Paul teaching about the kingdom of God in Rome. How is the growth of the early church like the parable of the mustard seed?

4. Read Mark 4:30–32. Why do you think Jesus didn't say anything about the sower? Who is the unnamed sower? What is our responsibility in advancing the kingdom? How would the parable of the mustard seed encourage

a person who is involved in a new ministry or one that is small?

5. Read Luke 13:18–19; Ezekiel 31:1–14; and Revelation 5:8–10. If the imagery of birds nesting in the branches of the mustard tree represent the inclusion of all nations in the kingdom, how does this parable affect your view of the church's responsibility to proclaim the gospel to the world?

6. Read Mark 4:30–32 and Mark 1:14–19, 40–45. How does the ministry of Jesus embody the truth of the parable?

Personal Application

7. Though the parable is about the growth of the kingdom, how would you use this parable to encourage growth in a new Christian? How does this parable encourage your growth?

8. Read Mark 4:30–32; Proverbs 14:29; and 1 Corinthians 13:4. In our present culture, most people want instant results. The Scriptures value patience. How does the parable of the mustard seed encourage patience?

||||||||||||||||||||||||||||| **Memory Verse** |||||||||||||||||||||||||||||

After this I looked, and there before me was a great multitude that no one could count, from every nation, tribe, people and language, standing before the throne and before the Lamb. They were wearing white robes and were holding palm branches in their hands. And they cried out in a loud voice:
"Salvation belongs to our God,
who sits on the throne,
and to the Lamb."

Revelation 7:9–10

The Children
in the Marketplace

Matthew 11:16–19; Luke 7:31–35

AUTHOR'S TAKEAWAY: *Pay attention to children;*
we can learn a lot from them.

We can learn a lot from children. For example, one of the best-known children's songs is rich with theology.

> Jesus loves the little children,
> All the children of the world.
> Red and yellow, black and white,
> They are precious in his sight.
> Jesus loves the little children of the world.

Jesus uses a children's song to describe how *this generation*, especially the religious leaders, responded to the ministry of John the Baptist and his ministry.

> "We played the pipe for you,
> and you did not dance;
> we sang a dirge,
> and you did not mourn."
>
> Matthew 11:17

And then, after briefly describing the ministry of the Baptist and his own ministry, Jesus concludes with a cryptic statement about wisdom, personified as woman.

> But wisdom is proved right by her deeds.
>
> Matthew 11:19

Jesus and John

After ministering to prepare Israel for the coming of the Messiah, John was arrested by Herod Antipas. While in prison, John sent his disciples to find out if Jesus was actually the promised Messiah. Jesus told John's disciples to tell John about the miracles they had witnessed, because they were proof Jesus was the Messiah (Matthew 11:1–6).

Jesus then turned to the crowd and publicly praised John (Matthew 11:7–10). He said John didn't come to win a popularity contest. Unlike the religious leaders who were easily influenced by public opinion, John was not a flimsy reed blowing in the wind. He didn't wear expensive clothes to impress people; instead, his clothing was made of camel hair, and he wore a crude leather belt. His message was blunt: He told people to confess their sins and repent. If they did, he baptized them. He was rugged but humble. His message wasn't about himself; he pointed to the one coming after him. "After me comes the one more powerful than I, the straps of whose sandals I am not worthy to stoop down and untie." He proclaimed good news but also warned of judgment: "I baptize you with water, but he will baptize you with the Holy Spirit" (see Mark 1:7–8; Luke 3:16–17).

Jesus said that the prophets had anticipated the coming of John the Baptist.

> I will send my messenger ahead of you,
> Who will prepare your way before you.
>
> Matthew 11:10; see also Malachi 3:1

John was the last of the Old Testament prophets but not the least. Jesus said that no one is greater than John the Baptist. But then he made a puzzling statement that seems contradictory to his praise for John: "Yet whoever is least in the kingdom of heaven is greater than he" (Matthew 11:11). This would include thieves, tax collectors, and even prostitutes. What? How is it possible that criminals and outcasts are greater than John? Jesus explains. John was a transitional prophet. His ministry was a divide between two eras of God's kingdom program. In the era of the law and the Prophets, people could only look forward to the time of fulfillment. But the coming of Jesus inaugurated a new era of the kingdom, so even the least in the kingdom had the unique privilege of realizing kingdom blessings, something that previous generations could only hope for. Those who believed John and trusted in Christ as Messiah and Savior experienced a new relationship with God—one based on love, not law. God was their Father, not lawgiver. They had far greater blessings—the full forgiveness of sins, the permanent gift of the Holy Spirit and his transforming work, lasting peace, and the hope of eternal life.

Note on Matthew, verse 12: The meaning of Jesus' reference to violence and violent people could be interpreted either negatively or positively. The NIV translates verse 12 negatively: "From the days of John the Baptist until now, the kingdom of heaven has been subjected to violence, and violent people have been raiding it." The other option is to translate the verse positively: "From the time of John the Baptist until now, the kingdom of heaven has been forcefully advancing, and people have been aggressively entering it" (my paraphrase). The negative view is consistent with the context if the parable is interpreted as a reference to the opposition that both John and Jesus experienced.

As further evidence of the arrival of the kingdom, Jesus says that John was the fulfillment of the expectations for the return of Elijah (see Malachi 4:5). John's ministry was like Elijah's, who warned Israel to repent. Jesus concludes with an exhortation: "Anyone with ears to hear should listen and understand!"

(Matthew 11:15 NLT). Jesus then tells the story of the children in the marketplace.

Children at Play

When I was a young boy, we didn't have electronic gadgets like kids have today. We didn't even have television. That's how old I am. But that wasn't a problem. All the kids in the neighborhood played together. One summer we built an elaborate fort in a vacant lot. I lived in the Southwest, where the soil is sandy and soft, so we were able to dig multiple connecting trenches and tunnels. We used cardboard and wood to support the tunnels. One group dug from one side, and another group worked from the other side. The plan was to meet in the center of the lot. I don't remember if we ever finished the fort, but that was okay. The fun was in building it. The effort ended when school started.

Jesus tells a story of children playing a game in the marketplace to explain the paradoxical responses to John and himself. To get other children to play, one group proposed a song for a wedding and then a song for a funeral. One was happy; the other sad. But it didn't matter. When they played the wedding song, the other children didn't dance. And when they sang a funeral song, the other children didn't mourn.

Though John and Jesus were contemporaries, their lifestyles and ministries were different. Jesus' ministry was more upbeat and jubilant. He began his ministry in Galilee at a wedding, where he turned hundreds of gallons of water into wine. Though he announced the coming of the kingdom, he was rejected. His opponents claimed that he was a glutton and a drunkard, and they ridiculed him for associating with sinners. John's ministry was more solemn. He was somewhat of an ascetic, who lived and ministered in the wilderness and ate locusts and honey. To prepare Israel for the coming of the Messiah, he challenged people to confess their sins and get baptized, or face the fires of judgment. Like Jesus, he was rejected. His critics charged he was demon possessed.

Jesus' point in the parable is that the contrasting styles of John and himself didn't make a difference. The Jews were obstinate and rejected both he and John, even though their styles were totally different.

Note: There is a question on the identity of the children playing the two songs. Do they represent the contrasting styles of Jesus and John, or do they represent the complaints of the Jews? Evangelical scholar and author Darrell Bock believes the introductory reference to "this generation" favors the latter. He says that "this generation" refers to the Jews, who complained that neither John nor Jesus met their expectations. They wanted John to lighten up, but he refused to abandon his austere lifestyle. And they wanted Jesus to be more legalistic, but he rejected their hypocritical piety and practiced a radical inclusivism that infuriated his critics. Bock concludes, "The messengers of God will not follow the people's tune, so Jesus accuses the generation of being like a bunch of complaining brats."[1]

The wisdom saying is slightly different in Matthew and Luke. In Matthew, Jesus concludes, "But wisdom is proved right by her deeds" (Matthew 11:19). Luke records a more personified statement, "But wisdom is proved right by all her children" (Luke 7:35). The point is basically the same. Though different than what was expected, wisdom will be proved right by the ministries of John and Jesus. Both fulfilled Old Testament promises.

REFLECT

1. What are some of the "complaints" (reasons) that people give today for rejecting Jesus?

2. Why was the use of a parable about songs from children playing in the marketplace an effective way for Jesus to describe his critics?

3. Read Mark 1:1–8. How did John prepare Israel for the coming of the Messiah? What are some of the ways that we can prepare people to receive Christ as their Savior?

(Include in your answer matters of both lifestyle and message.)

4. John's critics complained that he was too serious and judgmental, and Jesus' critics that he was too lenient and tolerant. How can we maintain a balanced Christian life that avoids a stern and rigid legalism and an indiscriminate licentiousness?

5. Read 1 Corinthians 9:19–23. How does Paul use his freedom to share the gospel with as many people as possible? To what extent should we adapt our lifestyle to changing cultural norms?

6. Read Luke 5:27–32. Why did the religious leaders complain to Jesus' disciples? What are some of the ways we can go out of our comfort zone to witness to others?

7. Read Luke 15:1–2. How did the response of tax collectors and sinners support Jesus' statement about wisdom?

8. Read 1 Corinthians 2:1–5. How does Paul's ministry and message in Corinth correlate with the wisdom statement in the parable? How does this passage encourage you in sharing your faith with unbelievers?

9. What new insight has this parable given you on how unbelievers respond to the gospel?

|||||||||||||||||||||||||||||||||| **OPTIONAL** ||||||||||||||||||||||||||||||||||

1. Which of the following do you think is the preferred view on the identity of the children?

   a. The children represent John and Jesus, who had different ministry styles, but both were rejected and criticized.

   b. The children are the Jews who wanted John and Jesus to change their ministry styles.

   c. What difference do each of the views make in the interpretation of the parable?

||||||||||||||||||||||||||||||| **Memory Verse** |||||||||||||||||||||||||||||||

Read and meditate on Proverbs 8, where "wisdom" is personified as a woman making an appeal for all to receive the gift of wisdom. You may want to memorize one or two verses from the chapter.

Jesus and Beelzebul, the Strong Man, and Good and Bad Trees

Matthew 12:22–37

AUTHOR'S TAKEAWAY: *Words matter.*

Most Americans don't think much about the devil or demons. I doubt if many even believe that there is a devil. It was different in first-century Palestine. People were keenly aware of the spiritual realm and lived in fear of evil spirits. Mark records that when Jesus began his ministry in Galilee, he was confronted by a demon in the synagogue at Capernaum (Mark 1:21–28). Luke records that the Ephesians burned their books on magic when they became believers—books that were worth a small fortune in today's currency (Acts 19:17–20).

The parable of the strong man is in the context of a sinister attempt to discredit Jesus and malign him as a servant of Satan.

Jesus and Beelzebul

Jesus didn't come to overthrow the Romans; he came to overthrow Satan. As evidence that he had come to establish God's kingdom, he forgave sins, healed people of their diseases, and cast out demons. The religious establishment, however, didn't like Jesus. He challenged their authority and condemned their hypocrisy. They set a trap by bringing to him a demon-possessed man who was also blind and unable to talk. They apparently thought that Jesus could not possibly help a man with multiple problems. But Jesus healed him and delivered him from demon possession. Unable to deny what Jesus had done, they accused him of using the power of Beelzebul. Beelzebul was the name for the Canaanite god of healing, but had become a code name for Satan by the first century (Matthew 12:22–24; 2 Kings 1:2).

A Preposterous Charge

Jesus said their accusation was preposterous. It was ridiculous to think that Satan would wage war on his own empire. Second, he asks them about the power of Jewish exorcists. Are they too empowered by Satan? Their charge is not only foolish, it is inconsistent (Matthew 12:25–27).

The Power of Jesus

Jesus says that his power to drive out demons by the Spirit of God is evidence of the presence of the kingdom of God. The expression "the kingdom of God has come upon you" does not mean Jesus' religious opponents were in the kingdom of God. It means that Jesus' power was evidence that the kingdom was a present reality.[1] The brief parable about the strong man reinforces Jesus' mission to overthrow the kingdom of Satan. Only someone who is stronger can rob the house of a strong man (Matthew 12:29). The implied point is that Jesus is stronger than Satan.

A Frightening Warning

Jesus says there are only two choices: "Whoever is not with me is against me" (Matthew 12:30). He then warns the religious leaders of what is known as the unpardonable sin. It is not a specific sin that is worse than all others. Because his miracles were by the power of the Holy Spirit, to deny his miracles is to blaspheme against the Spirit. One may be uncertain about Jesus' claim that he was the Son of Man, but there is no excuse for denying the evidence of the Spirit's power (Matthew 12:31–32).

Good and Bad Trees

Jesus abruptly changes the imagery when he says that you can know a tree by its fruit. In an agrarian culture, Jesus' audience would have known exactly what he meant. Jesus mixes metaphors, and calls the religious leaders a brood of vipers. The religious leaders are not merely mean-spirited; they are evil. Their accusations against Jesus are from the very core of their being—their hearts. They might fool people, but they cannot fool God. On judgment day, their words will either acquit them or condemn them (Matthew 12:33–37).

||||||||||||||||||||||||||||||||||||| **REFLECT** |||||||||||||||||||||||||||||||||||||

1. Read Matthew 12:22–24. Why do you think that most evangelical Christians in America pay so little attention to the spiritual realm? Do you think we should be more aware of the spiritual conflict between God and Satan? Why or why not?

2. Read Matthew 12:28. Since Jesus isn't in our midst driving out demons, what is the evidence today of the Spirit at work in the world?

3. Read Matthew 12:29 and Ephesians 1:18–23. If Christ is stronger than Satan and has incomparable power over

all the powers in the universe, should we as believers fear
Satan and his demonic henchmen? Why or why not?

4. Read Matthew 12:29 and James 4:7. How does the short
   parable of the strong man give you confidence to with-
   stand Satan and evil spirits?

5. Read John 16:7–11. What is the work of the Spirit in relation to unbelievers? Is it possible for unbelievers to resist
   the Spirit?

6. Read Matthew 12:31–32. Can we know if someone has
   committed the unpardonable sin? How? Have you ever
   encountered a person you think has committed the unpardonable sin?

7. Read Matthew 12:33–37 and James 3:7–12. What imagery
   does James use to warn us of the potential for good or
   evil of our words? How do our words reveal what is in our
   heart? What can we do to better control our tongue?

Memory Verse

Therefore God exalted him to the highest place
   and gave him the name that is above every name,
that at the name of Jesus every knee should bow,
   in heaven and on earth and under the earth,
and every tongue acknowledge that Jesus Christ is Lord,
   to the glory of God the Father.

Philippians 2:9–11

The Hidden Treasure and the Pearl of Great Price

Matthew 13:44–46

AUTHOR'S TAKEAWAY: *Sometimes we're just lucky. Or is it really luck?*

Jesus began his ministry by announcing the arrival of the kingdom of God. He challenged people to repent, to turn away from their old life, and to enter into a new life of blessing. People in Jesus' day were like us: When we hear of a fantastic offer, the first thing we want to know is how much it will cost.

The parables of the hidden treasure and the pearl of great price reveal how much it costs to gain entrance into the kingdom. It is clear from Jesus' teaching that you can't buy a ticket for the kingdom of God. Jesus teaches that a person must be willing to give up everything for the kingdom.

In the Gospel of Luke, we have a story about one of the few people who met Jesus and went away disappointed. His story is a marked contrast to the men in the parables of the hidden treasure and the pearl of great price. When Jesus was teaching about discipleship, a wealthy ruler asked, "What must I do to inherit eternal life?" (Luke 18:18). The ruler was an honorable man and told Jesus he had not committed any major crimes. Perhaps he thought he was already approved for eternal life. Jesus commended him, but said he lacked one thing. "Sell everything you have and give to the poor, and you will have treasure in heaven. Then come, follow me" (Luke 18:22). Unfortunately, he walked away from Jesus sad because he was "very wealthy" and was unwilling to give up his wealth (Luke 18:23).

These parables reflect real life circumstances in Jesus' world. The man who found the hidden treasure was probably a field hand. It's unlikely he was digging in another man's field. He was most likely working for the land owner when he accidently discovered a buried treasure. Throughout Israel's history, the land had been overrun by invading armies. When there was a threat of invasion, people would often protect their treasure by burying it in the ground. And even when there wasn't a threat, some would hide their valuables underground.

Pearls were highly valued by the wealthy in the first century, and the merchant (jeweler) was an astute businessman. Unlike the field hand, who accidentally found the buried treasure, the merchant was actively searching for the perfect pearl.

The Incomparable Value of the Kingdom

Both parables begin with the standardized formula, "The kingdom of heaven is like . . ." Though the two parables are different, they are best interpreted as a unit because they emphasize the same point. Both reveal the incomparable value of the kingdom.

In Matthew's Gospel, as Jesus continues his teaching on the different dimensions of the kingdom, he emphasizes that the kingdom cannot be purchased. It is of incomparable value, but anyone, rich or poor, can enter the kingdom. What one needs to do is let go of what they treasure in this world and surrender their life to

Christ. The two stories are not primarily intended to be persuasive; instead, they reveal the infinite value of kingdom membership.

Like today, whatever was found on a property belonged to the owner, so instead of telling the owner when a worker discovered a buried treasure, he sold everything to buy the field. Some think there is an ethical problem in the story because the worker didn't tell the owner, but the focus of the parable is on the infinite value of the kingdom. To find hidden meaning in the actions of hiding the treasure after it was found, the experience of joy after his discovery, and what he did to purchase the field would turn the parable into an allegory. They are features to enhance interest in the story. And though Jesus teaches that one must give up or at least be willing to give up everything to follow him, by itself the parable is not making the point that discipleship requires total abandonment. The main point is the kingdom is more valuable than any earthly possession.

Finding "a pearl of great price" was not an accident. Like today, pearls were highly valued and used in necklaces. A merchant was searching for quality pearls. Though he was a businessman, when he found an exceedingly valuable pearl, he didn't have enough money to purchase it. Like the worker in the field, he had to sell everything to buy it. The point is not that a person can buy membership into the kingdom like you would do to join a club; the parable reemphasizes the infinite value of the kingdom. Though he was wealthy, the merchant had to sell everything to buy the perfect pearl.

By Chance and a Diligent Search

We should not look for hidden meaning in the details of these two parables. Both make the same point about the matchless value of the kingdom. I think, however, we can also make a valid point about how the worker and the merchant found the kingdom: the worker found the buried treasure by chance; the merchant found the perfect pearl after a diligent search. **Point: People discover the kingdom in different ways.**

1. Why should or shouldn't we question the ethics of the worker who hid the treasure after he found it? What is the main point of the parable?

2. Read Ephesians 2:6–10. Though the two parables describe individuals who sold everything to purchase the kingdom, why is it impossible to buy or work your way into the kingdom?

3. Read Colossians 1:3–5, 13–14. How does a person enter into the kingdom of God?

4. The two parables reveal two different ways people discover the kingdom—one by chance (unintentional) and the other by a diligent search (intentional). Note the circumstances of the following individuals. Was their encounter with Christ intentional or unintentional?
   a. John 3:1–9—Nicodemus
   b. Acts 3:1–10—the handicapped man
   c. Acts 9:1–9—Paul

5. What were the circumstances of your coming to faith in Christ? Was it intentional or unintentional?

6. Read Luke 18:18–23. In the story of the rich young ruler, Jesus tells him to sell everything and give to the poor. Do you think Jesus' command is a universal requirement, or did Jesus know that the young man's love for money was an obstacle to his loving God and others? What are some of the earthly possessions that prevent people from trusting Christ as Savior (entering into the kingdom)?

7. Like the worker and the merchant, what did you give up to enter into the kingdom?

8. How do the following passages complement the two parables?

   a. Philippians 3:8–9

   b. Second Corinthians 4:16–18

   How do these passages encourage you as a Christ follower?

9. Read Matthew 6:33. Though the worker and the merchant sacrificed everything for the kingdom, what does Jesus promise for those who make the kingdom of God their highest priority? How does your life reflect the matchless value of the kingdom? What changes do you need to make to prioritize the kingdom?

|||||||||||||||||||||||||||||||||| **Memory Verse** ||||||||||||||||||||||||||||||||||

But seek first his kingdom and his righteousness, and all these things will be given to you as well.

Matthew 6:33

The Consummation of the Kingdom

The Fish Net

Matthew 13:47–51

AUTHOR'S TAKEAWAY: *Bad fish can't become good fish, but "bad" people can become "good" people.*

I've done a lot of fishing. Never with a net, but that's how they fished in Jesus' day. The net had corks on the top, weights on the bottom, and ropes on the four corners to drag it through the water. Because the net trapped all kinds of fish, the fishermen had to separate the good from the bad once the net was dragged on shore.

Several of Jesus' followers were fishermen and would have known immediately what Jesus meant when he told the parable of the dragnet, and even those who were not fishermen would have understood.

The parable of the dragnet comes at the end of the seven parables in Matthew 13. It serves as a conclusion to Jesus' teaching on the kingdom of heaven.

He Cast His Net

When fishing with a net, the fisherman would cast his net from a boat or the shore and pull it in, trapping fish of all kinds. He hoped most were good to eat, but he had to separate the good from the bad. He kept the good and threw the bad away.

The parable of the dragnet focuses on what the fisherman did with fish after he caught them, not how he caught them; Jesus uses the process of separating the good from the bad to teach what will happen at the consummation of the kingdom. Like the fisherman, angels will gather and separate the righteous (the good) from the wicked (the bad). The reference to angels in the time of judgment is consistent with what Jesus taught in his message about the coming of the Son of Man (Matthew 24:1–51; Mark; Luke). He predicted that when the Son of Man returns, he will send his angels to gather the righteous (Matthew 24:30–31). Part of the gathering process will be separating the righteous from the wicked.

The parable is about the kingdom of heaven, not the church, though the church is the community of God's people on earth with the responsibility for advancing the kingdom of God on the earth. But as stated previously, the church and the kingdom of God (heaven) are not the same, so the parable is not about separating true believers from professing Christians in the church. The parable is about separating believers from unbelievers in the world, when the Lord Jesus returns to establish his eternal kingdom of righteousness and peace. The reference to a blazing furnace, where there will be weeping and gnashing of teeth is standardized imagery to describe the fate of the wicked (see Matthew 13:42; 13:50; 24:51).

The parable has obvious parallels to the parable of the wheat and the weeds (Matthew 13:24–30, 37–43). Both emphasize the ultimate blessing of the righteous and the judgment of the wicked. It's not our responsibility to separate people; that's what the Lord will do at the end of the age.

Make Disciples of All Nations

What Jesus taught was consistent with what the prophets envisioned in the Day of the Lord. They anticipated the deliverance and blessing of God's people (Israel) and the judgment of their oppressors (the wicked) when the Lord established his kingdom (Isaiah 35:1–10; Joel 3:1–3; Amos 9:7–15). This unfortunately developed into an extreme nationalism and hatred for other nations. Jesus' association with Gentiles and others whom pious Jews considered sinners was shocking; it was one of the primary reasons many Jews concluded Jesus could not possibly be the Messiah. For Jews, the separation would be primarily between godly Jews and ungodly Gentiles.

The surprising aspect of the parable for first-century Jews would have been the reference to "all kinds of fish" (Matthew 13:47). The Greek word for *kind* is *genos,* which is also used for an ethnic group of people: *race.* Jesus is implying that his disciples have a responsibility to preach the gospel to the world. It is significant that the Gospel of Matthew ends with the Great Commission, "go and make disciples of all nations" (Matthew 28:19). As Jesus commanded, we are to be "fishers of people" (Mark 1:17 NET). There should be absolutely no racial, economic, or gender barriers that hinder us in proclaiming the Good News to all. God loves the world—not a select group or race of people—and so should we (John 3:16).

REFLECT

In thinking about the fact that "all kinds" of fish were caught in the net, answer the following questions.

1. The focus of the parable is not on separating the good from the bad during the growth of the kingdom, but on final judgment at the consummation of the kingdom.

   a. Who does the separating?

   b. Read Romans 1:16–20. What is the basis for distinguishing the righteous from the wicked? *Suppress the truth!*

    c. What are the parallels between this parable and the parable of the sheep and the goats (Matthew 25:31–46)?

    d. How do the parables of the dragnet and the sheep and goats refute universalism—the belief that everyone will eventually be saved?

2. Read Acts 1:8. How has this parable changed your thinking about our responsibility to witness to the world?

3. Read Acts 11:19–21. When the church was scattered by persecution, some of the believers courageously crossed racial barriers and preached the gospel to Greeks (Gentiles). What are the racial, economic, and gender barriers your church must overcome to proclaim the gospel to the world? How does this parable affect how you view people in your community who are marginalized?

4. Bad fish can't become good fish, but bad people can become good. How? See 1 Corinthians 1:26–31; 1 Thessalonians 1:9–10. How has your faith in Christ changed your life?

5. How has this parable changed your view of the growth and consummation of the kingdom?

|||||||||||||||||||||||||||||||| **Memory Verse** ||||||||||||||||||||||||||||||||||

Therefore, if anyone is in Christ, the new creation has come: The old has gone, the new is here!

2 Corinthians 5:17

The Wise and Foolish Virgins

Matthew 25:1–13

I grew up in a single-parent family. My father abandoned us when I was two. My mother raised me, but there were many who helped. I will never forget when an older man once told me, "Don't ever miss an opportunity!" That simple principle has served me well. I'm sure I've missed a lot of opportunities, but I've also taken advantage of many to make the most out of my life.

The parable of the ten virgins is about missed opportunity.

Note: The term *virgins* has different connotations today than in Jesus' day, so I usually substitute (not always) *young women* for *virgins*. Some commentators substitute *bridesmaids*, but that doesn't seem appropriate since they accompany the groom not the bride.

A First-Century Wedding

Weddings were extravagant occasions in Judaism and very different from weddings today. After a period of betrothal, which was far more binding than an engagement and could be broken only by a certificate of divorce, a date was set for the wedding. Invitations were sent out and preparations were made. The ceremony was not in a synagogue but in the home of the bridegroom. The bridegroom went to the home of the bride and escorted her to his home, where friends and family had gathered for a celebration that could last as long as a week. No one knew exactly when the groom would arrive, but it was usually in the evening, so it was important for the young women to be alert and prepared with lighted torches to escort the groom. When the bride and groom arrived, the wedding party and the guests celebrated with music, dancing, and a feast; the bride and groom were treated like royalty. The parable of the ten virgins (young women) is about the lost opportunity to enjoy the wedding festival.

Not Even the Son of Man

This is not the only reference to a wedding in the Gospels. Jesus and five of his disciples attended a wedding in Cana of Galilee (John 2:1–12), and Jesus used the analogy of a wedding to describe the generation that rejected him and John the Baptist (Matthew 11:16–19). Jesus also used the imagery of a wedding in the parable of the man who was thrown out of the wedding celebration because he wasn't properly dressed (Matthew 22:1–14).

The parable should be interpreted in the context of Jesus' teaching about future events in the Olivet Discourse (Matthew 24:1–36). In answer to the disciples' questions about the "signs" and "time" of Jesus' return, Jesus assured them of his return but said no one knows the exact time, "not even the angels in heaven, nor the Son, but only the Father" (Matthew 24:36). The parable of the ten virgins follows two short parables that teach diligence in waiting for the Lord's return. Because no homeowner knows when a thief might break into his house, he should be alert at all times (Matthew 24:42–44); and the second is an encouragement for responsible stewardship and a stern warning for irresponsible management. If a wealthy homeowner goes on an extended trip and puts one of his servants in charge, he will reward the servant if he is diligent in managing the household. But if the owner returns unexpectedly and discovers that his servant has been reckless and self-indulgent, he will severely punish that servant (Matthew 24:45–51).

The belief that Jesus taught about his future coming is confirmed by Paul's letters to the Thessalonians. He assures believers that they should not grieve for those who have died as those who have no hope, because Jesus rose from the dead and will one day return for both the dead and the living (1 Thessalonians 4:1–18). He urges them to be vigilant so they are not caught by surprise when the Lord returns (1 Thessalonians 5:1–12). In his second epistle to the Thessalonians, Paul assures believers that the Lord will judge their enemies when he returns, and assures them that the Day of the Lord has not come (2 Thessalonians 1:3–2:12).

Wise and Foolish

In anticipation of the arrival of the groom at the bride's house, ten young women were waiting with torches and were expected to escort the couple to the groom's house for the wedding festival. The torches were oil-soaked cloths on poles, and since they didn't know the exact arrival time of the groom, the young women should have brought extra oil to keep the torches burning. Five were wise and were prepared with jars of oil to keep their torches burning; five were foolish and did not bring extra oil. Some have suggested the oil is a symbol for the Holy Spirit and the lamps for good works, but to give symbolic meaning to the details of the parable turns it into an allegory. The oil and the torches are essential elements of the wedding story.

When the groom didn't arrive as expected, the foolish young women asked the wise young girls for oil. The five wise refused, and told the five unwise to go buy oil. Unfortunately, while the foolish young women were trying to buy oil, the groom arrived. The five wise women were rewarded for their diligence, and accompanied the groom to the festival. Once the door was shut, the unwise were locked out. Darrell Bock notes that locking the door was countercultural, but this is not unusual in parables because they often have a surprising twist. Typically, the door would have been left open for a wedding celebration.[1] Though the unwise pleaded for the Lord to open the door, he refused. And in another surprising twist in the parable, he said, "I don't know you" (Matthew 25:12).

"Lord, Lord"

His statement is important for understanding what is meant by *preparedness*. Some have suggested "preparedness" is the gift of the Spirit, and as mentioned, interpret the oil as a symbol for the Holy Spirit. The foolish young women are told to go buy oil, but to buy the Spirit would be to commit the sin of Simon, who tried to buy the gift of the Spirit (Acts 8:18–23). What it means to be prepared is suggested in the pleading of the foolish young women and the reply of the Lord: "'Lord, Lord' they said, 'open the door for us!' But he replied, 'Truly I tell you, I don't know you'" (Matthew 25:11–12). Those who are prepared to enjoy the blessings of the kingdom are those who have an authentic relationship with Jesus Christ. In "the Good Shepherd Discourse," Jesus said, "I am the good shepherd; I know my sheep and my sheep know me" (John 10:14). The foolish are those who do not know the Lord.

Jesus concludes with a point of application: "Therefore keep watch, because you do not know the day or the hour" (Matthew 25:13).

|||||||||||||||||||||||||||||||||||||| **REFLECT** ||||||||||||||||||||||||||||||||||||||

1. Why do you think the young women are described as *wise* and *foolish* rather than *prepared* and *unprepared*?

2. How are the customs of the wedding described in the parable similar and different from weddings today?

3. Weddings were obviously important in Judaism.

   a. Do you think formal weddings with a reception (celebration) are important today? Why or why not?

   b. What are some of the positive values of a formal wedding?

   c. It is common and acceptable today for couples to live together. How would you counsel them about the importance of a formal wedding?

4. Though the main point of the parable is about being prepared for the Lord's return, the principle of preparedness applies to many life experiences. In my first homiletics (preaching) class, my professor said, "We should always be ready to preach, pray, or die! So, if you are ever unexpectedly asked to preach, pray and see what happens!" How do you prepare for an important event? Can we prepare for unexpected events? If so, how?

5. The foolish young women were unable to borrow oil from the wise. When I was teaching I used to tell students that they wouldn't become godly merely because they were at Moody Bible Institute. Godliness is a virtue you must acquire for yourself. What are some of the other virtues of character that cannot be borrowed? How do you nurture your spiritual growth as a follower of Christ?

6. The point of this parable is more than a warning about missing a wedding celebration. Though all the young women were essentially the same, the separation of the ten into two distinct groups had eternal consequences—either entering the kingdom or being forever locked out. Why is it urgent that people prepare in advance for the return of Christ, and what would you tell them they should do?

But you aren't in the dark about these things, dear brothers and sisters, and you won't be surprised when the day of the Lord comes like a thief. For you are all children of light and of the day, we don't belong to darkness and night. So be on your guard, not asleep like the others. Stay alert and be clearheaded.

1 Thessalonians 5:4–6 NLT

The Sheep and the Goats

Matthew 25:31–46

AUTHOR'S TAKEAWAY: *Sheep on the right; goats on the left.*

It has been suggested that Jesus' extended teaching related to the short parable of the sheep and the goats gives the essence of what it means to be a Christian. Jesus said, "Truly I tell you, whatever you did for the least of these brothers and sisters of mine, you did for me" (Matthew 25:40). This would have been a radical message for Jesus' Jewish audience. The Pharisees taught that though the Jews were God's chosen people, they still needed to earn God's favor through strict obedience to the law of Moses.

Jesus undoubtedly surprised his audience with a new standard of judgment when he shifted the issue from keeping the law to helping people. He predicted that all humanity will be divided into two groups—one destined for eternal blessing, and the other for eternal judgment. And the basis for the separation is what we do for others. His claim that charity for others is the same as giving to Jesus is a surprising revelation of what it means "to be ready" for the Lord's coming. Though Jesus begins with the parabolic imagery of a shepherd separating sheep from goats, instead of developing the shepherd imagery, he continues his teaching with a second image—the direct dialogue between a king and his subjects.

Shepherds and Sheep

Shepherds had a tough job. They had to feed, water, and protect sheep from predators—a 24/7 job. To watch his flock during the day, the shepherd combined the sheep and goats, but at night he had to separate the restless goats from the sheep. Because goats tended to wander, he would place them in a pen while the sheep were left outside. It was not always easy to distinguish the sheep from goats. Though sheep are generally white, some are darker with markings similar to goats. But the shepherd knew his sheep, and they would listen to his voice when he called them at night.

Jesus uses the shepherd imagery to symbolize dividing humanity on judgment day. Because sheep are more valuable than goats, the sheep are placed on the right of the shepherd—the place of prominence. The goats are placed on the left—the place of disgrace. No reason is given for the distinction.

One "Like the Son of Man"

The identification of Jesus as the Son of Man comes from Daniel's dream about God's everlasting kingdom. Daniel describes one like "a son of man." "He was given authority, glory and sovereign power; all nations and peoples of every language worshiped him. His dominion is an everlasting dominion that will not pass away, and his kingdom is one that will never be destroyed" (Daniel 7:14). The New Testament confirms Jesus' authority to judge the nations. The angels praise him as the victorious Lamb who is worthy to receive praise, honor, and glory forever (Revelation 5:9–14).

Because the shepherd is the Son of Man, the abrupt shift from shepherd imagery to a king with authority to judge makes sense.

In the dialogue between the king and his subjects, Jesus gives the reason for the separation of the righteous and the wicked. Those who have had compassion on the needy are invited into the kingdom. The surprising aspect of Jesus' teaching is the identification of himself with the needy. When the righteous asked for a reminder on when they helped him, the Lord replied, "Truly I tell you, whatever you did for one of the least of these brothers and sisters of mine, you did for me" (Matthew 25:40).

In contrast to the righteous, who are blessed because they have helped those identified with Jesus, the wicked are those aligned with "the devil and his angels," and are judged because of their callous disregard for those needing help (Matthew 25:41). In this, his final parable, Jesus concludes with a summary of the contrasting destiny of the wicked and the righteous.

In Matthew 24:33, Jesus answered his disciples' questions about the end of the age and his return. The Son of Man will return in power and glory to reward the righteous and judge the wicked.

"The Least of These"

Jesus' teaching raises two significant questions. First, what does Jesus mean by "the least of these brothers and sisters of mine"? In Matthew 10:40–42, Jesus says that welcoming one of his disciples is the same as welcoming him, and identifies his disciples as "little ones." He again refers to his disciples as "little ones" in Matthew 18:6, 10, and 14. Though Jesus does not state that he is specifically referring to his followers (disciples) rather than people generally, it seems probable that is what he means in the broader context of Matthew. Jesus also identifies believers as "little ones" in Mark 9:42. Second, what is the criterion for blessing and judgment? It seems that Jesus' emphasis on "acts of kindness" is a contradiction to Paul's insistence on salvation by faith and not works. Jesus does not reveal the motivation for helping the needy, but if the reference is to Jesus' disciples, then it is those who believe in Jesus who are willing to help his disciples. So then, works of kindness are the result of faith in Jesus. The perspective on faith and works in the Epistle of James supports this view, "In the same way, faith by itself, if it is not accompanied by action, is dead" (James 2:17).

|||||||||||||||||||||||||||||||||||| **REFLECT** ||||||||||||||||||||||||||||||||||||

1. Read Matthew 25:34–46. Why do you think Jesus referred to helping others as the basis for final judgment?

2. Do you think as believers we have the responsibility to help people generally as well as other believers? Why or why not?

3. Read Matthew 25:37–39; Matthew 6:4. One commentator has called this "unconscious giving" because those helping the needy did not realize they were giving to Jesus. What are the advantages and disadvantages of remaining anonymous when giving?

4. Read Matthew 25:35–36. What are the six kinds of help listed in these verses? What are some of the other ways we can help the needy?

5. Read Philippians 4:14–16. How did the Philippians help Paul?

6. Read Acts 4:32–37. What did the early church do to help the needy? This kind of giving was not forced redistribution of wealth but charity of the heart. How does this kind of giving exemplify what Jesus taught in this passage?

|||||||||||||||||||||||||||||||||||| **OPTIONAL** ||||||||||||||||||||||||||||||||||||

1. As previously stated, most interpret "the least of these" to refer to Jesus' disciples, but some believe the passage supports a Christian "social responsibility" to provide

help for anyone in need. What are some of the benefits of Christians helping anyone in need? What are some of the risks of helping anyone who asks for help?

|||||||||||||||||||||||||||||||||| **Memory Verse** ||||||||||||||||||||||||||||||||||

And God's grace was so powerfully at work in them all that there were no needy persons among them. For from time to time those who owned land or houses sold them, brought the money from the sales and put it at the apostles' feet, and it was distributed to anyone who had need.

Acts 4:33–35

The Ethics
of the
Kingdom

Discipleship

The Tower Builder and the Warring King

Luke 14:25–35

AUTHOR'S TAKEAWAY: *Don't assess your worth by how much you possess but by how much you have given away.*

When I was a new Christian, one of my favorite songs was "I Have Decided to Follow Jesus." The words are simple but powerful: "I have decided to follow Jesus; no turning back." They capture Jesus' message on discipleship.

If someone had told me I would have to hate my father and mother and bear a cross to become a Christ follower, I don't think I would have become a Christian. But that's exactly what Jesus told those following him as he made his way to Jerusalem.

The Cost of Following Jesus

Large crowds were following Jesus on his final journey to Jerusalem. Some were perhaps thrill seekers, hoping for an entertaining miracle. Others expected Jesus to overthrow the Romans and become king. Knowing what they were thinking, Jesus made it clear what it would take to follow him. He is totally honest in setting forth the demands of discipleship, and refutes the notion of "easy believism." Following Christ requires uncompromising devotion.

Jesus began with startling statements on the high cost of discipleship. He illustrates his teaching with the parables of the tower builder and the warring king (Luke 14:28–33). Following the two parables, Jesus concludes his teaching with an illustration (parable) of salt (Luke 14:34–35). Because the parables are part of Jesus' teaching on discipleship, we will examine the entire section.

The Family and the Cross (Luke 14:25-27)

A first-century Jew would have readily identified with the two metaphors used—the family and the cross. One was a symbol of love and devotion; the other of suffering and death. Like some cultures today, nothing was more valued than family relationships. So it would have been shocking when Jesus said that unless you hate your father, mother, wife, children, brothers, and sisters you could not be his disciple. The term *hate* is relative, not absolute. The requirement for following Jesus is to love him more than anything, even one's family.

The second metaphor moves beyond loving devotion to the ultimate sacrifice. The cross was a symbol of suffering and death. The Jews were painfully aware that the Romans executed people by crucifying them on a cross, and every Jew would have understood what Jesus meant when he said you cannot be my disciple unless you carry your cross. Condemned criminals were forced to carry the cross beam to the place of execution. Obviously dead people can't follow Jesus, so his challenge was to die to self. When Jesus arrived in Jerusalem, he did not organize an army to overthrow the Romans. He was arrested, tried, and crucified. Few in the crowd anticipated what happened to Jesus and were willing to surrender their life to him.

To illustrate his teaching on radical love and total commitment, Jesus tells two short stories.

A Foolish/Dumb Builder (Luke 14:28-30)

A man decided to build a tower. A tower wasn't like the giant skyscrapers for our modern cities; it was a watchtower for alerting a city of an approaching enemy or thieves coming to raid a vineyard. The builder wasn't very smart. He started building but hadn't thought about cost, so he didn't have enough money to finish. When it became known what had happened, people mocked him, saying, "This person began to build and wasn't able to finish" (Luke 14:30). We don't pay much attention to people who go bankrupt today. If anything, we feel sorry for them. But in an "honor/shame" culture, this would have been disastrous. The man would have been broke and shamed. Jesus' point is obvious. People need to carefully consider the cost before following Jesus.

A Wise/Smart King (Luke 14:31-32)

Jesus says that before a king declares war on another king, he will consider his chance of winning. If he has only ten thousand troops and the other king has twenty thousand—a two to one advantage—the first king will seek peace rather than defeat. The point is similar to the parable of the foolish builder but does not include the demand for radical discipleship.

Some have identified one or the other of the kings as God, but that seems unlikely. New Testament scholar Craig Blomberg states that it is inconceivable that if God is identified as the first king, he would consider surrendering; if he represents the second king, it is unreasonable to think that Jesus is encouraging people to consider their chance of defeating God before making a decision to follow him.[1]

91

The point is best understood in relation to the tower builder. He was foolish; the king was wise. Those who want to follow Jesus should thoughtfully consider what that means so that their decision does not end in a humiliating defeat.

A Realistic Warning (Luke 14:33)

By warning about the high cost of discipleship, Jesus isn't trying to discourage people from becoming disciples, but he is realistic and honest. Jesus is fully aware of his destiny. In the upper room on the night he was betrayed, Jesus warned the Twelve: "Remember what I told you: 'A servant is not greater than his master.' If they persecuted me, they will persecute you also" (John 15:20). Here he tells the large crowd what is ultimately required of a Jesus follower: "Those of you who do not give up everything you have cannot be my disciples" (Luke 14:33).

Saltless Salt (Luke 14:34–35)

Luke records Jesus' warning about "unsalty" salt to conclude Jesus' teaching on discipleship. His teaching could be considered a short parable, but it is probably best to consider it an illustration. Either way, it is a warning. Fortunately for people like me, Jesus wasn't trying to teach a chemistry lesson.

Jesus uses salt as an illustration in two other contexts. In the Sermon on the Mount, Jesus says that like salt, believers should have a preserving impact in a decaying world (Matthew 5:13). Jesus warns about causing others to stumble, and urges his followers to be peacemakers. If they can't do that, how will they be salt in the world (Mark 9:50)?

Here Jesus warns about failing to respond to his teaching. If salt is separated from the impurities in it, the residue is useless and can only be thrown away; it can't be used as fertilizer for the land or as compost in the dunghill. "Whoever has ears to hear, let them hear" (Luke 14:35). Those who reject Jesus and his teaching will be cast away. They are as useless as "unsalty" salt.

1. When you became a believer, did you realize the high cost of following Jesus? How has your understanding of what it means to be a Christian changed since you first trusted Christ as Savior?

2. Read Luke 14:25–27. The term *hate* is obviously relative and not absolute. How does the term reflect priorities in one's devotion to Christ?

3. What does *cross-bearing* mean for you?

4. Read Matthew 9:57–62. Do you think that in the Matthew passage and in this passage Jesus is discouraging people from following him? Why or why not?

5. What is the difference in how these two parables emphasize thoughtful consideration of a commitment to follow Christ?

6. How would you use these two parables to explain to a prospective believer the importance of "counting the cost" before trusting Christ as Savior?

7. Read Revelation 2:1–7. What happened to the church at Ephesus? What are some of the worldly ambitions and/or possessions that distract us from becoming fully devoted followers of Christ? How do you nurture your love and devotion to Christ?

8. How have these passages changed your understanding of what it means to be a fully devoted follower of Christ?

1. There are different views about whether or not a person only needs to trust Christ as Savior to become a Christian,

or if they need to commit fully to the demands of discipleship. How would you apply the teaching in these two parables to salvation and discipleship? Note: It is a debate that is not easily resolved.

2. Do you think the preaching/teaching of television evangelists reflects Jesus' teaching on discipleship? Why or why not?

############################### **Memory Verse** ###############################

Then Jesus said to his disciples, "Whoever wants to be my disciple must deny themselves and take up their cross and follow me. For whoever wants to save their life will lose it, but whoever loses their life for me will find it."

Matthew 16:24–25

The Shrewd Manager

Luke 16:10–15

AUTHOR'S TAKEAWAY: *"Tell the truth, or at least don't lie."*—JORDAN PETERSON

While writing on Jesus' parables, I have also been reading *12 Rules for Life* by Jordan Peterson. Rule 8 is "Tell the truth, or at least don't lie." The dishonest manager in Luke should have read Peterson's book. It would have saved him a ton of grief and those of us trying to understand the story a lot of difficult interpretative questions. The story of the shrewd manager is the most puzzling of Jesus' parables. It presents an apparent ethical problem because Jesus seems to use the actions of a dishonest business manager to teach a positive lesson about stewardship.

"They Loved Money"

Luke 15 contains Jesus' response to the criticisms of the religious leaders that he welcomed tax collectors and sinners with three parables. In the parables of the lost sheep, the lost coin, and the prodigal son, Jesus emphasizes the love of God for the kind of people the Pharisees despised. Jesus then turns to his disciples and teaches them about stewardship. His teaching is a further rebuke of the Pharisees, "who loved money" (16:14), but also a challenge for believers on the management of resources for matters of eternal importance (16:9).

"He Was Dishonest"

A wealthy businessman discovered that his manager was dishonest. When the manager was asked to give an account of his management, he knew he would be fired, so he called in the debtors. He asked them how much they owed and then reduced their debts, reasoning they would care for him in the future. He reduced the debt of the debtor who owed nine hundred gallons of wine by 60 percent, and the man who owed a thousand bushels of wheat by 20 percent. Instead of rebuking his manager, the businessman commended him because he had acted "shrewdly" by making friends for the future.

Jesus makes two additional applications of the parable. He says that those who can be trusted with a little can be trusted with much (16:10–12). And as a direct rebuke of the religious leaders, he says no one can serve two masters. If you love one, you will hate the other. "You cannot serve both God and money" (Luke 16:13).

"He Was Shrewd"

The parable is a realistic scenario of what could have happened to a dishonest manager. As today, the wealthy would often hire a financial manager to take care of his assets. The rich man, however, when he discovered his manger was cheating him, asked to see the books and told him he was fired.

The manager faced a dilemma. He was not fit to work and didn't want to beg, so he decided to do a huge favor for his master's debtors: He greatly reduced their debts.

The reduction of debt can be interpreted in two ways: he was reducing the actual debt plus interest, which would have been a loss for his master, or he was reducing the debt by the amount of his commission, so he lost money but his employer didn't. Those who find it problematic that Jesus would use a story about dishonesty to teach about stewardship favor the second interpretation. There is nothing in the story that suggests this interpretation, so others believe the message is related to his prudence in preparing for the future and not his dishonesty.

When his employer found out what he had done, he commended him for his shrewdness. Another question is whether the parable ends with verse 8 or 9. If it ends at verse 8, then Jesus makes three different but related applications of the parable. But the reference to "master" in verse 8 and the expression, "I tell you," at the beginning of verse 9 favors Jesus' application beginning with verse 9.

Jesus does not allegorize the details of the parable; rather he makes three applications all related to "unrighteous mammon." *Mammon* is a general term used for worldly possessions, not specifically money. *Money* is not inherently evil, but it can easily be misused. First, the money manager was shrewd because he used worldly wealth to prepare for eternity. This is not "works salvation," but using one's wealth as evidence for authentic faith. Second, trustworthiness in small accounts demonstrates the ability to manage larger accounts. This is true in finances and the spiritual realm. Jesus said, "But store up for yourselves treasures in heaven, where moths and vermin do not destroy, and where thieves do not break in and steal. For where your treasure is, there your heart will be also" (Matthew 6:20–21). How we spend our time and money reveals what we truly value. Third, Jesus blindsided the Pharisees when he said that it is impossible to serve two masters. A person will either hate the one but love the other or love one but hate the other; we cannot love both God and money.

1. How does the parable encourage integrity?

2. Read Proverbs 10:9. How does the parable illustrate the truth of Proverbs 10:9?

3. Read Titus 2:6–8. Why is integrity important to our witness for Christ?

4. Read Luke 16:3–7. Do you think there is an ethical problem if reducing the debts of those who owed money to his employer is interpreted as another act of dishonesty? Why or why not?

5. Read Luke 16:9. How can we use our material possessions to help other people?

6. Read Luke 16:10–12. What is one aspect of your life where your faithfulness in a small matter has led to responsibility in larger matters?

7. Read Luke 16:13.

   a. Why is it impossible to serve two masters?

   b. What are some of the ways we can test our love for God?

8. Read 1 Timothy 6:6–10.

   a. What is contentment? How can we develop an attitude of contentment?

   b. Why is contentment more important than material possessions?

   c. How is the love of money the source of all kinds of evil?

9. Read 1 Timothy 6:17–19.

   a. What is Paul's command to the rich?

   b. How does his teaching about the use of material possessions support Jesus' teaching in the parable?

############################## **Memory Verse** ##############################

No one can serve two masters. For you will hate one and love the other; you will be devoted to one and despise the other. You cannot serve God and be enslaved to money.

Luke 16:13 NLT

The Talents

Matthew 25:14–30

AUTHOR'S TAKEAWAY: *"We get our money the old-fashioned way. We earn it!"*—SMITH BARNEY AD, 1981

When I was in high school I began saving for college. I had a paper route during the school year and worked full time in the summer. I put all of my money in a savings and loan institution. I don't remember how much I had saved, but in my junior year I was devastated when I received a letter from the state of Arizona informing me that the IRS had taken control of the institution because of mismanagement of funds. I was told to take my savings book to the local office to collect a percentage of my savings. After standing in a long line, I finally made it to a teller. They looked at my deposit book and calculated my refund. I got about $25, only enough to pay the application fee to the university. I didn't know what to do because I had lost all the money I'd saved for college. But I was determined and continued working my senior year, and saved enough money to at least get started at the university.

The parable of the talents is about investing for the future, and what happened to one man who didn't invest his talent. It is the second parable Jesus used to conclude his sermon on his second coming. In the parable of the ten young women (virgins), Jesus stressed readiness. In this parable, he explains what it means to be ready.

Rewards and Punishment

A wealthy man planned an extended trip. Since he wouldn't be able to manage his wealth while traveling, he entrusted his money to three of his servants. He gave the first servant five talents; the second, two; and the third, one. The master was not discriminating against his servants by giving them different amounts. The phrase "Each according to his ability" indicates the distribution was according to what each could effectively manage. Plus, in the application of the parable, the amount is insignificant. What matters is what the servants did with their talents.

The term *talent* in the parable means something totally different than it does today. We use the term to refer to a natural aptitude or special ability that a person has acquired. In the parable, it refers to an enormous sum of money. One silver talent was equal to six thousand denarii; a gold talent would have been worth thirty times that much. It has been estimated that one talent would be the wages of a day laborer for thirty years. Jesus is obviously using hyperbole (exaggeration) for the amount of money given to each of the servants. See Matthew 18:24 NASB for a similar use of *talent* in the parable of the unforgiving servant.

In the absence of their master, the first two servants invested and doubled their money. The third buried his in the ground. From the parable of the hidden treasure, we can assume that burying treasure in the ground was one way of keeping it safe. The first two were obviously confident of their master's return and were willing to take risks to make a profit. The servant who buried his talent in the ground apparently hoped to claim it if his master didn't return.

Though he is gone for a long time, the master eventually returns. When the first two give an account of what they had done with their talents, the master commends them, "Well done, good and faithful servant!" He promises them even greater responsibility in the future and invites them to celebrate with him.

The meeting between the master and the third servant did not go well. He brought his master the one talent he had received, claiming that he did this because he knew that his master was harsh and demanding. He was afraid to risk losing it, so he hid the talent in the ground. The statement, "I knew that you are a hard man, harvesting where you have not sown and gathering where you have not scattered seed" (Matthew 25:24), was either a compliment of his master's shrewd business practices or a criticism of his unethical business practices. His reasoning makes sense in a volatile economy, but not in the kingdom of God. He had undoubtedly heard the positive commendation of the other two servants and expected the same. And the listening audience probably did as well. So both the servant and the listeners would have been shocked by the master's response. He said the servant was wicked and lazy—wicked because he hoped the talent would become his if his master didn't return, and lazy because he wasn't willing to put in the effort needed to make a profit on an investment.

To reinforce a principle that my wife often repeats, Jesus ordered the talent be given to the servant who had ten. And then he said, "For whoever has will be given more, and they will have an abundance. Whoever does not have, even what they have will be taken from them" (Matthew 25:29). My wife puts it like this: "The rich get richer, and the poor get poorer." What is true in economics is also true in the realm of the kingdom. The third has become "the odd man out," and has nothing. But it is even worse. Jesus condemns him: "And throw that worthless servant outside, into the darkness, where there will be weeping and gnashing of teeth" (Matthew 25:30). He not only loses everything but is sentenced to eternal punishment.

The third servant was obviously an unbeliever. Though some think he was a "professing believer," I don't think so. The distinction is based on faith. The servants who truly believed in the return of the master did their best to faithfully serve their master. As Paul says in Ephesians 2:8–10, we are saved by faith, and also saved to do good works. Works do not save us but are the evidence of genuine faith. The third servant did nothing to advance the kingdom of God because he was spiritually bankrupt.

############################## **REFLECT** ##############################

1. One commentator stated that the parable of the talents confirms a universal principle of growth. "Here we are face to face with a great and important truth—in life we can never stand still; if we are not going forward, we must go backward. We must see to it that every day we are advancing, know something new, do something a little better."[1] In what areas of your life does this parable motivate you to grow?

2. Read 2 Peter 1:5–11. (Please read this passage in the New Living Translation, if possible.)

   a. Why does Peter say we should be growing in these Christlike virtues?

   b. What spiritual disciplines do you practice to grow as a Christian?

   c. What does it mean "to be ready" for the Lord's return?

3. Why do you think the third servant buried his "talent" rather than invest it? What is the lesson for believers today?

4. Read Mark 4:24–25. How does giving the third servant's talent to the servant who had ten emphasize responsible stewardship?

5. What does the way "the master" (the Lord) treated the three servants reveal about the character of God?

6. Do you believe you are ready for the Lord's return? Why or why not?

|||||||||||||||||||||||||||||| **Memory Verse** ||||||||||||||||||||||||||||

The righteous are rewarded with good things.

Proverbs 13:21

The Unforgiving Servant

Matthew 18:21–35

AUTHOR'S TAKEAWAY: *Don't be mean to others, especially those who are nice to you.*

We don't know much about Lamech. There's a short account of his hateful and vengeful spirit in Genesis (Genesis 4:17–24). He was the seventh from Adam in the lineage of Cain. He was rebellious and arrogant. He married two wives contrary to God's design for marriage, and boasted how he had taken revenge on a man who had attacked him. "If someone who kills Cain is punished seven times, then the one who kills me will be punished seventy-seven times!" (Genesis 4:24 NLT). Lamech's terrifying boast shows the dangerous consequences of sin. Unfortunately, there's a little bit of Lamech in all of us. We're not murderously violent, but when offended, it's much easier for us to retaliate than to forgive.

Knowing that it's our nature to get even rather than forgive, Jesus focused on forgiveness as one of the primary signs of God's grace in the parable of the unforgiving servant.

Matthew doesn't tell us why Peter asked a question about forgiveness. Peter knew as a Jew that he was expected to forgive others, but now as a follower of Christ he wondered how often he should forgive. He no doubt thought his suggestion of seven times was more than adequate, so Jesus' answer must have been shocking. "I tell you, not seven times, but seventy-seven times" (Matthew 18:22). In contrast to Lamech's boast of unlimited vengeance, Jesus taught unlimited forgiveness.

Forgiveness

In economics, forgiveness is the canceling of debt owed. In the spiritual realm it is the canceling of the debt of sin. In the parable of the unforgiving servant, Jesus uses a story of debt to teach about forgiveness. Jesus emphasizes the importance of tangible evidence of transformation in those who profess faith in him as Savior. Those who have truly experienced forgiveness are willing to forgive others.

The parable consists of three scenes (acts) and a conclusion.

Act One: A King and His Debtors (Matthew 18:23–27)

A king decided to audit his debtors. His accountant discovered that one debtor owed him ten thousand talents (millions of dollars)—an amount that could never be repaid. The king ordered that the man, his wife, his children, and all of their possessions be sold to repay the debt.

The man pleaded for more time to repay the debt. Instead of giving him more time, the king had pity on him and canceled his entire debt.

Act Two: A Man and His Debtors (Matthew 18:28–31)

The man left but came upon another man who owed him a hundred denarii (only a few thousand dollars)—an amount that could conceivably be repaid. The man who had been forgiven was brutal to his debtor. He grabbed the debtor by the throat and demanded repayment. Just as he had asked the king for more time, the debtor fell down on his knees and begged for more time. But instead of showing mercy as he had received, he had the man arrested and imprisoned. Prisons were harsh places. The cells were more like dungeons. They were dark and unsanitary, and prisoners were often tortured.

Act Three: The King and the Man (Matthew 18:32–34)

The man's unforgiving treatment of the debtor was made public and troubled some of the king's servants. They were outraged and told the king what the man had done. The king was angry and summoned the man. He rebuked him. "You wicked servant, I canceled all of that debt of yours because you begged me to. Shouldn't you have had mercy on your fellow servant just as I had on you?" (Matthew 18:32–33). The king handed the man over to jailers to be tortured until he paid all he owed, which was impossible.

The Heavenly Father (Matthew 18:35)

Jesus concludes the parable with a warning. "This is how my heavenly Father will treat each of you unless you forgive your brother or sister from your heart" (Matthew 18:35).

God's Love and Mercy

The parable is a powerful story about God's infinite love and mercy. There's no debt of sin so great that God won't forgive a truly repentant sinner. The Cretans were notorious for their dishonesty and brutish lifestyle. One of their own prophets described their animal-like behavior: "Cretans are always liars, evil brutes, lazy gluttons" (Titus 1:12). But God's grace was far greater than their sin; some had trusted Christ as their Savior. Paul gives a wonderful summary of God's mercy and grace. "But when the kindness and love of God our Savior appeared, he saved us, not because of the righteous things we had done, but because of his mercy. He saved us through the washing of rebirth and renewal of the Holy Spirit, whom he poured out on us generously through Jesus Christ our Savior, so that, having been justified by his grace, we might become heirs having the hope of eternal life" (Titus 3:4–7). To eliminate any doubt about his truthfulness, Paul states, "This is a trustworthy saying" (Titus 3:8). In other words, Paul is saying, "I am not lying. What I am telling you is the truth."

The second act of the parable is a warning. It is inconceivable how a true follower of Christ who had benefited from the abundance of God's grace could be so harsh and unforgiving. The unforgiving servant showed that his life had not been transformed by God's mercy. That was unfortunate. He may have thought the king would never find out how he had treated his debtor or that the king didn't care, but he was wrong.

The third act describes the terrible consequences of having been offered forgiveness but remaining unrepentant. Other servants were so offended they could not keep silent. They told the king what the unforgiving servant had done. God, of course, doesn't need anyone to tell him about the affairs of humanity. Paul reminds us that God knows our hearts. "Nevertheless, God's solid foundation stands firm, sealed with this inscription: 'The Lord knows those who are his,' and, 'Everyone who confess the name of the Lord must turn away from wickedness'" (2 Timothy 2:19). The unforgiving servant underestimated the king and forgot that though the king is merciful, he is also just. By spurning God's love and mercy, he had condemned himself. The king ordered him thrown into prison and tortured. The imagery is metaphorical for hell. Hell is not a place where unbelievers will be with their friends; it is a place to be avoided because separation from God is the ultimate disaster.

How Do You Want God to Treat You?

Jesus' concluding statement does not imply that we can somehow save ourselves by how we treat others. Rather, Jesus' point is that no true believer should ever be so unloving and hard-hearted that they are unwilling to forgive others. An unwillingness to forgive is evidence that a person hasn't truly accepted God's mercy. Because they have rejected the king, they are not fit for the kingdom.

REFLECT

1. In answer to Peter's question, what do you think Jesus taught about forgiveness?

2. Why do you think Jesus used a willingness to forgive as evidence of genuine faith? What is some of the other evidence of faith?

3. Why do you think the unforgiving servant was unwilling to forgive his debtor after the king had showed him abundant mercy? Why is it so difficult for us to forgive those who have offended us?

4. Read Psalm 101:1. How does the parable illustrate the two attributes (characteristics) of God David describes in this psalm? We're not God, but how can we balance these two attributes in our relationships with others?

5. Read Psalm 101:3. Do you think this verse describes the unforgiving servant? Why or why not? Why do you think David says we should avoid such people?

6. How does the amount the servant owed the king represent our debt of sin to God? Why is the debt of our sin infinitely greater than any monetary debt someone might owe to us?

7. Read 1 Timothy 1:12–14. How is Paul's attitude different from that of the unforgiving servant? How has this parable changed your attitude toward those who will inevitably offend you?

8. Read Psalm 103:12. How is our willingness to forgive others a witness to God's willingness to cancel the debt of sin?

9. Read Matthew 6:14–15. How does this parable help you understand what Jesus taught in the Lord's Prayer about forgiveness?

10. Read Matthew 5:7. How is the parable a commentary on Jesus' teaching in the Beatitudes? How does an unforgiving spirit show that we have never truly experienced God's mercy?

|||||||||||||||||||||||||||||| **Memory Verse** ||||||||||||||||||||||||||||||||||

I will sing of your love and justice;
To you, LORD, I will sing praise.

Psalm 101:1

The Watchful Servants and the Wise Manager

Luke 12:35–48; Matthew 24:45–51

AUTHOR'S TAKEAWAY: *Always do your best, even when no one is watching.*

I don't like waiting. I was never good at it, but my experience in the military made my impatience even worse. Our favorite slogan as recruits during basic training was, "Hurry up and wait!" And that's exactly what we did. During training, we marched double time from one location to another, and then we waited and waited and waited. So I blame my impatience on the army. It's their fault!

In the parables of the watchful servants and the wise manager, Jesus teaches us how to wait expectantly for his return.

Watchfulness

Some form of Jesus' teaching about watchfulness is recorded in all three Synoptic Gospels—Matthew, Mark, and Luke.

Mark concludes Jesus' message on the coming of the Son of Man with a short parabolic admonition on watchfulness (Mark 13:32–36). Because no one—not even angels or the Son, but only the Father—knows the exact time of the Lord's return, believers are admonished to keep watch. They should be especially alert during the night so no one will be caught sleeping. Jesus' exhortation is not only for the disciples but for everyone. "What I say to you, I say to everyone: 'Watch!'" (Mark 13:37).

Though the context is slightly different, both Matthew and Luke record the parable of the watchful and wise servant (Matthew 24:45–51; Luke 12:42–48). The context in Matthew is the same as the parabolic admonition in Mark. It is part of Jesus' admonition "to keep watch" because no one except the Father knows when the Son of Man will return (Matthew 24:36).

Luke records both the parable of the watchful servants and the wise servant as the answer to Peter's question on whether Jesus' teaching applied only to the disciples or to everyone.

For this study, we will confine ourselves to the two parables from the Gospel of Luke. Though it's only two verses, the parable of the thief at night is discussed in a separate study (Luke 12:39–40; Matthew 24:43–44). I recommend that you consider dividing this study into two sessions.

The Watchful Servants (Luke 12:35-38)

Though a large crowd was with him, Jesus spoke directly to his disciples (Luke 12:1, 22). He assured them that the Father would take care of them. They were of much more value than birds and flowers, so they shouldn't worry; instead, they should seek God's kingdom. He challenged them to give to the poor and to remember that their treasure was in heaven (Luke 12:22–33). What a person values is a matter of the heart. "For where your treasure is, there your heart will be also" (Luke 12:34).

Though their heavenly treasure was safe from the dangers of this world, the disciples would have to wait for it. That required patience since there would apparently be a long delay before the return of the Son of Man. To encourage his disciples to be ready, Jesus uses the analogy of servants waiting for their master to return from a wedding. The analogy is more of an extended metaphor than a parable, but that doesn't invalidate the point that Jesus wants his followers to be ready for his return, even if it is "in the middle of the night or toward daybreak" (Luke 12:38).

Note: The text literally reads "the second or third watch," which suggests the Lord's coming could be at night, when least expected (Luke 12:38, Greek). Luke was most likely using Roman rather than Jewish time.

REFLECT

1. Read Luke 12:35–38.
   a. What is the imagery Jesus uses to emphasize proactive waiting in anticipation of his return?
   b. What is unusual about the actions of the master when he returns from a wedding banquet?
   c. Read John 13:12–17. What did Jesus do for his disciples in the upper room that illustrates the reversal of roles in the parable?
   d. How does Jesus' willingness to humble himself to serve his disciples encourage you to serve others? Is there someone you can serve in your church or community?
2. Read 2 Peter 3:3–7. What is Peter's argument against scoffers who deny Christ's second coming?
3. How do we remain spiritually ready for the Lord's return?

The Wise and Wicked Managers (Luke 12:41-48)

Jesus' teaching about "preparedness" prompted Peter to ask, "Lord, are you telling this parable to us, or to everyone?" (Luke 12:41). Jesus doesn't answer Peter's question directly; instead, he describes the consequences of both faithful and unfaithful service in a parable about a manager.

A good manager is reliable even in the extended absence of his master. He cares about the other servants and provides for their daily needs. When the master returns, he will put that servant in charge of all his possessions because he has proven himself trustworthy in smaller matters

But in contrast, Jesus describes a manager who is irresponsible. In the lengthy absence of his master, he beats the other servants, both men and women. He is a glutton. He gorges himself with food and gets drunk. What will happen to a cruel and self-indulgent servant if his master returns unexpectedly? His master will cut him in pieces and send him to a place for the "unfaithful." The punishment is unbelievably harsh by modern standards, but was practiced in ancient warfare and in the punishment of criminals. It may be hyperbole, but it is still a warning of severe punishment. It is not clear in Luke's account if Jesus is referring to the severe discipline of believers or the eternal punishment of unbelievers. In Matthew's version, the imagery supports the final judgment of unbelievers. The wicked servant is assigned to a place with "hypocrites," "where there will be weeping and gnashing of teeth," a figure of speech for extreme suffering and regret (Matthew 24:51; cf. Mark 13:28).

So Be Trustworthy (Luke 12:47-48)

Luke gives an additional application, not recorded in Matthew, focusing on degrees of punishment. A servant who knows what he should do but doesn't will be more severely punished than a servant who doesn't do anything because he didn't know what to do. These verses clearly suggest degrees of punishment.

|||||||||||||||||||||||||||||||||||||| **REFLECT** ||||||||||||||||||||||||||||||||||||||

Though the parable is an admonition for all believers to conscientiously and compassionately serve others in anticipation of the Lord's return, what Jesus teaches is also applicable to the concept of "a servant leader." Jesus modeled servant leadership and encouraged the Twelve to follow his example (see John 13:1–17).

1. Read John 21:15–19.

    a. How does Jesus' reinstatement of Peter correlate with the service of the wise manager?

    b. What is the basis for Jesus' charge to Peter?

    c. Why is this an essential virtue for servant leaders and all believers?

2. Read 1 Peter 5:1–4.

    a. How does Peter identify himself?

    b. What imagery does he use to describe leaders (elders) in the church?

    c. What are the points of correlation with the parable?

    d. How will the Chief Shepherd (Christ) reward those who have served faithfully when he returns?

3. How does the parable suggest degrees of punishment and reward?

4. How does the parable relieve believers of any fear of unjust punishment?

5. How can we be faithful and wise as we wait expectantly for the Lord's return?

|||||||||||||||||||||||||||||||| **Memory Verse** ||||||||||||||||||||||||||||||||

May the Lord make your love increase and overflow for each other and for everyone else, just as ours does for you . . . and holy in the presence of our God and Father when our Lord Jesus comes with all his holy ones.

1 Thessalonians 3:12–13

The Thief

Matthew 24:43–44; Luke 12:39–40

AUTHOR'S TAKEAWAY: *If you live in Chicago, lock your doors at night.*

In some urban areas, crime is so high that almost all businesses and homeowners have taken measures to guard against thieves by installing cameras and alarms, and even putting bars on doors and windows.

My wife and I now live in Colorado near our grandkids, but we lived in the greater Chicago area and downtown Chicago for thirty-seven years. Early on we learned that it was absolutely necessary to lock your doors at night. When we lived in a complex of townhouses, several of our neighbors had a problem with burglars. One of the scariest was when one of our neighbors, a single woman, forgot to lock her back door. From her bedroom, in the middle of the night, she heard noise downstairs and realized that someone was rummaging around in her kitchen and living room. She didn't know what to do. Should she turn on the lights and scream? Try to quietly call 9-1-1? Or simply wait and hope the intruder would leave? She did the latter and was fine. Fortunately, nothing was stolen.

Crime isn't only a modern-day problem. Even under Roman rule, break-ins were common in first-century Israel. This prompted Jesus to make an unusual comparison of his second coming to that of a thief. If the homeowner had known when the thief was coming, he would have prepared, so Jesus says, "You must also be ready, because the Son of Man will come at an hour when you do not expect him" (Luke 12:40).

In his book *The Parables of Jesus*, David Wenham refers to stories like this one as crime parables. Other crime parables are the robbing of a strong man's house, the unjust judge, the dishonest money manager, and the parable of the pounds, where Jesus compares himself to an unpopular king (Mark 3:23–27; Luke 16:1–9; 19:11–27). Wenham argues that these kinds of stories are evidence for reliability of the Gospels because it is unlikely that the early church would have made up these stories if Jesus himself had not done so. He continues, "It is remarkable that Jesus draws on such a gallery of rogues to illustrate his ministry, but of course in none of the parables concerned is Jesus commending the morality of the characters concerned, but simply using lively stories to make his point."[1]

REFLECT

1. Read Matthew 24:43–44 and 1 Thessalonians 5:1–6.
   a. What imagery did both Jesus and Paul use to encourage believers to be ready for the Lord's return?
   b. Why did they use this negative imagery?
   c. What are the differences between the coming of Christ and a thief?
   d. What are the differences Paul describes between unbelievers and believers?
2. Read 1 Thessalonians 5:8–11. How does Paul say we should live while we wait for the Lord's return? What does

it mean to be sober? (Paul is not referring to substance abuse.) What else does Paul say we should do as we wait for the coming of Christ?

3. Read 2 Peter 3:10–13.

   a. What imagery does Peter use to describe the day of the Lord (includes Jesus' second coming)?

   b. What does Peter say will happen with the coming of the day of the Lord?

   c. How does he encourage us to prepare for that day?

   d. What does it mean to live a holy and godly life?

4. What have you done to protect your home from thieves? What have you done to make certain you are prepared for Jesus' second coming?

||||||||||||||||||||||||||| **Memory Verse** |||||||||||||||||||||||||||

Dear friends, now we are children of God, and what we will be has not yet been made known. But we know that when Christ appears, we shall be like him, for we shall see him as he is. All who have this hope in him purify themselves, just as he is pure.

1 John 3:2–3

Reversal

The Narrow Door

Luke 13:22–30

AUTHOR'S TAKEAWAY: *Don't cut in line, because the first will be last and the last first!*

To fulfill his mission as the Son of God and Savior of the world, Jesus ministered in Judea, Galilee, and even Samaria, but his ultimate destination was Jerusalem. It was there he would surrender his life as a sacrifice for the sins of the world. Luke tells us about Jesus' decision to go to Jerusalem. "As the time approached for him to be taken up to heaven, Jesus resolutely set out for Jerusalem" (Luke 9:51). It was not a surprising decision for Jesus, but it was for his disciples and those traveling with him. Jesus had encountered open hostility in Jerusalem. It was a place of danger. As somewhat of a preview of what would happen in Jerusalem, Jesus sent messengers ahead to make arrangements to stay in a Samaritan village. They were rejected. James and John, known as the sons of thunder for their fiery personalities, wanted to call down fire from heaven to destroy the village. Jesus rebuked them. He hadn't come to destroy people but to save them (Luke 9:52–54).

Because Jesus knew that he would be arrested and executed in Jerusalem, he began emphasizing the high cost of discipleship as

119

he continued toward Jerusalem (Luke 9:57–62). One perceptive individual traveling with him asked, "Lord, are only a few people going to be saved?" (Luke 13:23). Instead of a direct answer to the man's question, Jesus responded with the parable of the narrow door (Luke 13:22–30).

Only One Door

I have never lived in a house with only one door. Most homes in America have multiple doors, but many homes in first-century Israel were built with only one entrance. The parable explains what will happen to the invited guests at a banquet once the owner of the house has closed the door.

Locked Out

The parable is a warning. Jesus says that people should make every effort to enter the kingdom before it is too late. Once the host has closed the door, the invited guests will not be able to enter; no matter how much they plead, he will not open the door.

Those locked out represent Israel's religious leaders and others who had an opportunity to enter the kingdom but refused. Now it's too late. They claim they know the host. They ate and drank with him; he taught in their villages and towns. But their relationship was superficial. He denies that he knows them and sternly rebukes them, "Away from me, all you evildoers" (Luke 13:27).

Weeping and Gnashing of Teeth

Jesus gives a surprising twist to the story. Not only are the invited guests locked out, but they are in anguish because they will see others enjoying the messianic banquet with the patriarchs—Abraham, Isaac, Jacob, and the prophets. Others come from the four corners of the earth, which would undoubtedly include Gentiles and others despised by most Jews. Those who were outsiders are now insiders, and insiders have become outsiders.

First Last, Last First

A divine reversal has occurred. The last are now first, and the first are last. Why? What has happened? In the account that follows, Luke explains. He exposes Herod Antipas's plot to kill Jesus, reiterates Jesus' divine destiny in Jerusalem, shows Jesus' compassion for Jerusalem, and anticipates Jesus' second coming (Luke 13:31–35).

Why the reversal? Because Israel officially rejected Jesus, the offer of the kingdom is extended to all the earth. This is all according to God's sovereign plan of salvation for the world. Paul explains that in his incomparable wisdom, God has predetermined that Israel's rejection of the Messiah has given Gentiles the opportunity to believe, but that Israel will eventually recognize Jesus as their messianic Savior (Romans 9–11). And then they will sing, "Blessed is he who comes in the name of the Lord" (Luke 13:35). This is a pilgrim psalm that was sung by Jews on the way to Jerusalem that Jesus applies to his second coming.

|||||||||||||||||||||||||||||||||||||||| **REFLECT** ||||||||||||||||||||||||||||||||||||||||

1. Read Isaiah 25:6.
   a. What imagery does Isaiah use to describe God's kingdom? How does this parable complement Isaiah's imagery?
   b. Read John 2:1–12. How does Jesus' first miracle support the imagery of this parable as a description of the kingdom?
2. Read John 14:6 and Acts 4:11–12. How does this parable support Jesus' claim in John 14:6? In an age of religious

pluralism, what are some of the challenges of claiming that Jesus is the only way of salvation?

3. Read Luke 13:24. Who does the door represent? What do you think Jesus meant when he said people should "make every effort to enter through the narrow door"? What is our (human) responsibility in the salvation process?

4. Read Luke 13:26–27 and Matthew 7:21. What kind of relationship do those who were shut out claim to have with Jesus? Why is this inadequate? Are there people today who think they are saved but are not? What is the tragic mistake they have made?

5. Read Matthew 19:28–30. How could you use the principle of divine reversal to encourage those who are poor in material possessions or have been marginalized by the socially elite?

|||||||||||||||||||||||||||||||||||| **Memory Verse** ||||||||||||||||||||||||||||||||||||

As God's co-workers we urge you not to receive God's grace in vain. For he says,

> In the time of favor I heard you,
> and in the day of salvation I helped you.

I tell you, now is the time of God's favor, now is the day of salvation.

2 Corinthians 6:1–2

The Wedding Banquet

Matthew 22:1–14

AUTHOR'S TAKEAWAY: *RSVP, especially*
if you're invited by God.

My wife and I have been married for a very long time—so long
that I can't remember most of the details of our wedding. But I do
remember I was surprised (and a bit intimidated) by how many
people attended. My wife belonged to a large church, and her
family had a large network of friendships. We sent out hundreds
of announcements with an RSVP, and it seemed like everyone we
invited came. I can't imagine how disappointed Linda and I would
have been if we sent out hundreds of invitations and no one even
responded. But that's exactly what happened to a king who invited
guests to a wedding for his son. He sent his servants out with the
invitations, but all of the invited guests refused to attend. Some
even abused and killed the king's servants.

By What Authority

The parable of the banquet is the third in a series Jesus taught in
response to the priests and elders questioning his authority. After
he made his triumphal entry into Jerusalem, chased the money

123

changers out of the temple, and cursed a barren fig tree, Jesus began teaching in the temple. The religious leaders immediately challenged him. "By what authority are you doing these things?" they asked. "And who gave you this authority?" (Matthew 21:23). Jesus responded with the parables of the two sons, the wicked tenants, and the wedding banquet (Matthew 21:28–22:14).

A Banquet

Though many argue that the parables of the banquet in Matthew (22:1–14) and Luke (14:15–24) are different versions of the same parable, the differences are significant enough to believe that Jesus used banquet imagery for stories on two different occasions. The parable in Matthew is about a king, a royal wedding banquet, ungrateful guests who refused to attend, another invitation to anyone who was willing to attend, and a guest who came in his street clothes. In Luke, the parable is about a banquet (without specifying a wedding banquet), guests who made excuses for not attending, and a second and third invitation to the poor and handicapped.

As in the previous two parables, Jesus says that the parable of the banquet is about the kingdom of heaven (God), and uses banquet imagery to warn of the consequences for rejecting the opportunity to enter the kingdom. The three main "characters" in the parable are the host, those who reject the invitation, and those who accept a second invitation. The king who prepared a wedding banquet for his son is God. In the immediate context, those who refuse to attend the banquet are the religious leaders, but it could be anyone who ignores the kingdom invitation. The second group of invited guests is anyone, "the bad and the good," who responds to the invitation.

Many Are Invited but Few Are Chosen

Three unique features heighten the intrigue in the parable: 1) Because some of the original guests completely ignored the wedding invitation, and others even mistreated and killed the king's servants, the king sends his army to punish them and destroy their city; 2) One of the replacement guests shows up without the proper clothes and is thrown out into a place of darkness and pain; and 3) Jesus concludes with a cryptic (puzzling) theological statement, "For many are invited, but few are chosen" (Matthew 22:14).

Two Surprising Revelations

The parable contains two surprising revelations about entering into the kingdom. First, there is only one way into the kingdom, and God (the king) will judge those who deliberately ignore his invitation. Jesus made a similar point in the parable of the narrow door (Luke 14:22–30): He warned that once the door is closed, it will not be opened again (cf. John 14:4). Second, as in his other parables, Jesus emphasizes the theme of reversal. Jews who expected to enjoy kingdom blessings are replaced by those they despised—the poor, sinners, and most of all, Gentiles. The man without wedding garments is a warning about hypocrisy. God will welcome into the kingdom only those who have put on his righteousness through faith in his Son.

REFLECT

1. Note the imagery for God's rich provision of salvation in the following passages:
   a. Isaiah 25:6. How does Isaiah describe God's gracious and generous provision of blessings for the world?
   b. Mark 2:19–20. What imagery does Jesus use to describe the coming of the kingdom? What was the occasion for Jesus' first miracle (see John 2:1–12)?
   c. Revelation 19:9. How does the angel describe the final union between Christ and believers?

    d. Ephesians 1:3. Why is the imagery of a wedding banquet appropriate for describing the spiritual blessings God has lavished on us in Christ?

2. Read Matthew 22:1–2. In the ancient Near East, it would have been unthinkable to refuse an invitation to a royal wedding. What is the implication about the guests who refused the invitation?

    a. About their loyalty to the king?

    b. About their respect for his son?

    c. Who do the unresponsive guests represent in the parable?

    d. How are people today like the Jewish religious leaders?

3. Read Matthew 22:5–6. Why is it important for people to know the consequences of rejecting Christ?

4. Read Matthew 22:8–10.

    a. Who were the street people in Jesus' day? Who are the street people today?

    b. Why are street people typically more responsive to the gospel than religious people?

    c. How can the church today invite people, who are shunned by society, to come to Jesus?

5. Read Matthew 22:11–13. Most commentators agree that the man without wedding clothes was a hypocrite and insulted the king by his phony piety. He was without excuse. When asked why he didn't wear wedding clothes, "The man was speechless."

    a. Read Matthew 5:20, 21:31–32; Romans 1:16–17; and Ephesians 4:22–24. What do the wedding clothes represent?

    b. How are people today like the man who refused the wedding clothes provided by the king?

1. What happens to the racial, social, and economic differences that divide us when everyone is dressed in the same wedding garments—God's righteousness?

2. Read Matthew 22:14. Jesus' comment is often used to support the doctrine of election, but that may be reading more into the statement than Jesus intended. In the context of the controversy with the priests and elders, the focus of Jesus' statement is that all who are invited must come dressed in God's righteousness. This would have been a shocking rebuke of the self-righteous religious leaders who thought they could fool God with their hypocritical piety.

    a. What are the dangers of hypocrisy in the church today?

    b. How can we avoid hypocrisy in our relationship with Christ? What are the questions we can ask about our motives in worship, serving, giving, etc.?

|||||||||||||||||||||||||||||| **Memory Verse** ||||||||||||||||||||||||||||||

On this mountain the Lord Almighty will prepare
 a feast of rich food for all peoples,
a banquet of aged wine—
 the best of meats and the finest of wines.
On this mountain he will destroy
 the shroud that enfolds all peoples,
the sheet that covers all nations;
 he will swallow up death forever.
[Memorize this part:] **The Sovereign Lord will wipe away
 the tears
 from all faces;
he will remove his people's disgrace
 from all the earth.
The Lord has spoken.**

Isaiah 25:6–8

The Great Banquet

Luke 14:15–24; cf. Matthew 22:1–14

AUTHOR'S TAKEAWAY: *They all made excuses.*

For comic relief I sometimes read from a book titled *Anguished English*, written by Richard Lederer, who was a teacher for twenty-seven years in Concord, New Hampshire. In the chapter titled "Excuses, Excuses," he has listed some of the hastily written notes received from parents explaining their son's or daughter's absence from school.

Here are a few:

My son is under the doctor's care and should not take P. E. today. Please execute him.

Please excuse Mary for being absent. She was sick and I had her shot.

Please excuse Roland from P. E. for a few days. Yesterday he fell out of a tree and misplaced his hip.

John has been absent because he had two teeth taken off his face.

Please excuse my son's tardiness. I forgot to wake him up, and I didn't find him until I started making the beds.

128

And last but not least:

Maryann was absent December 11–16, because she had a fever, sore throat, headache, and upset stomach. Her sister was also sick, fever and sore throat, her brother had a low grade fever and ached all over. I wasn't the best either, sore throat and fever. There must be the flu going around school, her father even got hot last night.

We laugh at those excuses. They are funny! But excuses are not always a laughing matter. In the parable of the great banquet the excuses for not attending were not funny. They were lame and insulting to the host.

The Sabbath and a Man with Dropsy

The parable of the great banquet is one of several Jesus told on his way to Jerusalem (Luke 13:22). During his journey to Jerusalem, he focused on the high cost of discipleship and the countercultural nature of the kingdom.

Israel's religious and cultural "watchdogs" were closely watching Jesus when he was invited to the house of a prominent Pharisee. It was the Sabbath, and Jesus knew they were ready to pounce at the first opportunity. Seeing a man who was suffering from dropsy—a swelling of the arms and legs—Jesus asked a question that caught them by surprise: "Is it lawful to heal on the Sabbath or not?" Realizing it was a Catch-22, they refused to answer. Jesus healed the man, and then asked if the law permitted rescuing an animal on the Sabbath. Again, they refused to answer. Noticing the guests jockeying for the most prominent seats at the table, Jesus countered the conventional custom saying that if they want to be honored, they should take the lowest seat, and they would be honored when the host invites them to take a more prominent place. He shocked the host again when he told him that instead of inviting the rich, he should invite the poor and the handicapped.

No one apparently knew exactly how to respond to Jesus' startling countercultural assertions, so one of the guests hazarded what he thought was a pious remark. "Blessed is the one who will eat at the feast in the kingdom of God" (Luke 14:15). The man's comment reflected the prevailing belief that entrance into the kingdom was guaranteed for the pious like those present for the meal. Jesus responded with a parable warning those who objected to his radical teaching about the kingdom and his countercultural lifestyle.

A Banquet

The banquet imagery for the kingdom comes from the Old Testament. Isaiah prophesied about a new age when God will bless the righteous with a banquet for all the earth. "In Jerusalem [literally "on this mountain"], the LORD of Heaven's Armies will spread a wonderful feast for all the people of the world. It will be a delicious banquet with clear, well-aged wine and choice meat" (Isaiah 25:6 NLT). Two features of the imagery are important. The Lord himself is the host, and the invitation is universal. Though the invitation is universal, only those who have trusted in the Lord respond. "In that day they will say, 'Surely this is our God; we trusted in him, and he saved us. This is the LORD, we trusted in him; let us rejoice and be glad in his salvation'" (Isaiah 25:9).

Well in advance, the host sent out invitations for a banquet. It is important to remember that the host in the story represents God or perhaps his Son. On the day of the banquet, he sent his servants to personally inform all of the invitees who had responded to the first invitation that the feast was ready. It was customary to send invitations in advance so the host would know how much food to prepare for those who said they would attend. Three had previously said they would attend, but on the day of the banquet they made flimsy excuses for not coming. The three represent the wealthy guests at the house of the Pharisee and those who rejected Jesus and his invitation to enter the kingdom.

The reasons might seem valid on the surface, but they actually reveal contempt for the host. The first says, "I have just bought a field, and I must go and see it. Please excuse me." No one today would buy property without first seeing it, and no one would have in the first century. The second says, "I have just bought five yoke of oxen, and I'm on my way to try them out. Please excuse me." To pull a heavy wagon or plow in a field, oxen needed to pull together. No one would buy a team of oxen without first trying them out, just as no one today would buy a pickup or tractor without a test drive. His reason was another implausible excuse. The third man's response seems reasonable: "I just got married, so I can't come." He may have been telling the truth, but the problem is he had already accepted the invitation and presumably knew the date of his own wedding, which conflicted with the date of the banquet. Plus, two major events like a wedding and a banquet would not have been planned for the same time in a small village. Like the first two, his excuse was insulting.

When the servant returned and told his master how the invitees had responded, he was furious. He told the servant to go and invite the outcasts of Israel—the poor, the crippled, the blind, and the lame. Author Kenneth Bailey has observed the irony of the second group of invitees. He writes, "For centuries commentators have observed that the poor are not invited to banquets, the maimed do not get married, the blind do not go out to examine fields, and the lame do not test oxen."[1] The servant did as commanded, but there was still room for more guests. He sent his servant out a second time "to compel" more to come so his house would be full. The term *compel* (NIV) here means "to urge." As many have suggested, the second invitation extends the guest list beyond the ethnic and geographical boundaries of Israel, which many believe would include Gentiles. If so, the parable hints at the mission to the Gentiles—a mission that was carried out by the early church.

The parable ends with a chilling warning for those who despised Jesus: "I tell you, not one of those who were invited will get a taste of my banquet" (Luke 14:24). The warning may have been a direct statement by Jesus rather than part of the parable. In either case, it is a warning to anyone who rejects Jesus that they will not get into the kingdom simply because they are Jews or rich. The parable obviously has a broader application than only to the wealthy, but in the context of Luke, the parable is directed to those who loved money more than God. "The Pharisees, who loved money, heard all this and were sneering at Jesus. He said to them, 'You are the ones who justify yourselves in the eyes of others, but God knows your hearts. What people value highly is detestable in God's sight" (Luke 16:14–15). Jesus did not teach that poverty was a prerequisite to the kingdom, but that the economic poor were more likely to become spiritually rich. James warns the early church not to discriminate against the poor because they have a special place in the kingdom of God. "Has not God chosen those who are poor in the eyes of the world to be rich in faith and to inherit the kingdom promised to those who love him?" (James 2:5).

One might summarize the parable as those who are excluded from the kingdom have only themselves to blame.

|||||||||||||||||||||||||||||||||||||||| **REFLECT** ||||||||||||||||||||||||||||||||||||||||

1. When understood in their cultural context, the excuses were ridiculous and even insulting. What do the excuses of the invited guests reveal about their attitude toward Jesus and his invitation to enter the kingdom?

2. How would you feel if you planned a party and all the people you invited said they couldn't come?

3. Read Luke 14:18–23. At the beginning of the parable, Jesus identifies all the reasons for not attending the banquet as excuses. He then gives three examples of excuses for rejecting Jesus' invitation to enter the kingdom. What are some of the excuses people make today for rejecting Christ as Savior?

4. Read 2 Peter 3:8–9. How do you harmonize the teaching of this parable with Peter's statement that the Lord is patient and not willing that anyone should perish?

5. Because the original guests refused to come, the host ordered his servants to invite others. How should the host's actions affect our personal strategy and the church's strategy for reaching the lost?

6. What does extending the invitation to the "outcasts" in Israel reveal about God's concern for the lost? How has this aspect of the parable changed your attitude toward the poor, the homeless, and the handicapped?

7. Read Revelation 7:9–10. How is John's vision of those worshiping the Lamb a fulfillment of one aspect of the parable?

8. Read John 1:16–17. Since the replacement guests were poor and handicapped and could not possibly repay the host, what does this reveal about God's grace?

9. Read Acts 13:46–48. How does Paul's experience at Antioch fulfill the truths of this parable?

10. Read 1 Corinthians 11:17–34. How does Paul's teaching to correct problems at the Lord's Supper in the church at Corinth reflect the emphasis placed on economic and ethnic diversity in the kingdom of God?

Memory Verse

Don't be fooled by those who try to excuse these sins, for the anger of God will fall on all who disobey him.

Ephesians 5:6 NLT

The Rich Man and Lazarus

Luke 16:19–31

AUTHOR'S TAKEAWAY: *Don't wait—it may be too late!*

The parables of the shrewd manager and the rich man and Lazarus bracket Jesus' criticism of the Pharisees. Though the Pharisees claimed to love God, they loved money and sneered at Jesus for associating with the poor (Luke 16:14). Both parables warn about the danger of money. The unwise manager compromised his integrity by cheating his employer, and the rich man abandoned compassion for the poor for self-indulgence. The shrewd manager acted wisely by repenting and using his possessions to prepare for the future. The rich man died without repenting and experienced irreversible judgment.

Several features of the story of the rich man and Lazarus make it unique. First, because one of the characters is named, some think it's a real life story. However, the story has a parabolic beginning: "There was a rich man . . ." (Luke 16:19). And the naming of Lazarus strengthens the contrast between the rich and poor. Second, it is the only parable that describes circumstances both before and after death. Third, the story reverses the prevailing Jewish belief that wealth was evidence of blessing and poverty of judgment.

The Super Rich and the Dirt Poor

In This Life

The parable opens with a contrasting description of the rich man and Lazarus. His purple clothing and ostentatious feasting suggests the man was super rich. Purple dye was expensive and was used for the clothing of royalty and the extremely wealthy. Lazarus, whose name in the Hebrew means "God is my help," is the exact opposite. Much like Job, he is covered with ulcers, and rendered even more defiled by the dogs who licked his sores. William Barclay says that the rich used loaves of bread to wipe their hands and then threw the bread away.[1] Lazarus was waiting for chunks of bread, not bread crumbs.

In the Next Life

The scene shifts abruptly from this life to the next. We are not told how, but both Lazarus and the rich man die. Their fortunes are now reversed. Lazarus is carried by angels to Abraham's side (bosom). In Judaism, Abraham's bosom was the place of blessing. In the parable of the narrow door, there is "weeping and gnashing of teeth" when Jews see Abraham, Isaac, Jacob, and others enjoying a messianic banquet in the kingdom of God while they are excluded (Luke 14:28–29).

The rich man, in contrast to Lazarus, is in torment. Angels do not come for him; he is in Hades (hell). He sees Lazarus at a distance and recognizes him. The rich man, knowing of Lazarus's plight, had done nothing to help him. But now the rich man is the one begging for mercy. He asks Abraham to send Lazarus to quench his thirst. There is an element of sympathy in Abraham's reply. He addresses the rich man as "child"—a family term of

135

endearment—but says that it is impossible. The rich man's eternal destiny was determined by choices in his former life; plus, an impassible chasm separates him from Lazarus. We should avoid turning the parable into an allegory by interpreting literally the details of the parable. We can know there is life after death in either a place of blessings or judgment, that we will be aware of our circumstances, and that our destiny is determined by the choices we make in this life and is irreversible.

What about My Brothers

Unable to gain relief for himself, the rich man shifts his concern to his brothers. He asks Abraham to send Lazarus to warn his five brothers. Though not fully understood at the time, it would have been impossible for post-resurrection Christians to have missed Abraham's response as a veiled reference to the resurrection, and it is entirely possible in view of Jesus' teaching about his death and resurrection that some might have understood it at that time. Abraham replied that if a person didn't believe Moses and the prophets, then even if someone returned from the dead (a dramatic miracle), they wouldn't believe.

〰〰〰〰〰〰〰〰〰〰〰〰〰〰〰 **REFLECT** 〰〰〰〰〰〰〰〰〰〰〰〰〰〰〰

1. Read Psalm 112:1, 3, 9–10. What is the relationship between righteousness and our attitude toward the poor?

2. Read Proverbs 31:20. What is the difference between the godly wife and the rich man? How is she an example for us to follow? What is your attitude toward money, and how do you use your resources to help others?

3. Read Psalm 73. How does this parable illustrate the warning about envying successful (wealthy) people who reject God?

4. Read James 1:9–11; 2:1–7, 14–18. Apparently discrimination and neglect of the poor were problems in the early church. How does neglect of the poor expose defective faith? What are some of the ways your church helps the poor?

5. Read Acts 11:27–30. In a country that is as prosperous as ours, is it easy to pursue a self-indulgent lifestyle and ignore the poor? What are some of the ways that we can remain sensitive to the needs of others?

6. Read Proverbs 14:31. The man did not end up in Hades (hell) because he was rich. Money is not inherently evil. The issue was not wealth but what the rich man did and didn't do with his wealth. What does the use of our possessions reveal in our relationship with God?

7. Read Matthew 28:11–15. Why do you think Jesus said that if the man's five brothers didn't believe the Law and the Prophets (Scripture), they wouldn't believe even if someone returned from the dead? How is this prophetic of the response of Israel's religious leaders after the resurrection of Jesus?

8. Read Luke 16:29–31. Why do you think that people who do not believe what the Scriptures teach about Christ won't be convinced—even by the resurrection—to trust him as the Son of God and Savior?

|||||||||||||||||||||||||||||||||||| **OPTIONAL** ||||||||||||||||||||||||||||||||||||

1. How does this parable refute the belief that unbelievers will get a second chance after they die?

2. One popular view of eternal judgment is annihilationism (the total destruction of the wicked). What are some of the problems with annihilationism, based on the message of this parable?

3. A somewhat recent view argues that God's love wins in the end and that all people will be saved. What are the problems of that view, based on the warning in this parable?

IIIIIIIIIIIIIIIIIIIIIIIIIIIIIIIIII **Memory Verse** IIIIIIIIIIIIIIIIIIIIIIIIIIIIIIIIII

People are destined to die once, and after that to face judgment.

Hebrews 9:27

The Good Samaritan

Luke 10:25–37

AUTHOR'S TAKEAWAY: *Help those in need, no matter who they are.*

I have tried to be a Good Samaritan, but have not always been successful. Knowing when to help others is a challenge, especially in a big city like Chicago, where I lived for thirty-seven years. Because a lot of the street people want money for stuff other than food, it is difficult to know when and how to help.

One afternoon, after teaching and encouraging students to be compassionate and generous, I took off on my bike for a ride on the lakeshore path that runs for thirty miles along Lake Michigan. About five miles into my ride I smelled a foul odor, and then I saw him—a homeless man. He had built a shelter beside the path with plastic and cardboard. His stuff was piled everywhere. He looked terrible and smelled really bad. I thought about stopping but didn't. I flew by on my bike to get away from the stench as quickly as possible. But I couldn't leave my conscience behind. I had just taught students about compassion, and I didn't even stop to find out if I could help. *Well,* I said to myself, *I'm only a few miles from my turnaround point; I'll stop on my way back.* But when I came back, the homeless man was gone. I am still troubled by that missed opportunity. I could and should have been a Good Samaritan but wasn't.

Who Is My Neighbor?

Since the time of the church fathers, parables have suffered from the abuse of allegorical interpretations. Blomberg gives an extended example of Augustine's allegorizing of the parable of the good Samaritan: "The wounded man stands for Adam; Jerusalem, the heavenly city from which he has fallen; the thieves, the devil who deprives Adam of his immortality; the priest and the Levite, the Old Testament law which could save no one; the Samaritan who binds the man's wounds, Christ who forgives sin; the inn, the church, and the innkeeper, the apostle Paul."[1]

To avoid highly imaginative interpretations, it is essential to pay attention to the reason Jesus told the story of the Good Samaritan. Like the parable of the unjust servant, Jesus told the parable as an answer to the question of a scribe (a legal expert on the law).

What Must I Do to Inherit Eternal Life?

The story begins when the scribe asks Jesus a question. He addressed Jesus as "teacher" because he apparently respected him as a competent scholar; however, his question was to test Jesus. He wanted to find out how well Jesus knew the law. The question was not about a trivial matter. He asked, "What must I do to inherit eternal life?" Jesus spoke about "eternal life" on other occasions (see Matthew 19:16; Luke 18:18; John 3:14–16). It was basically a question about salvation, which most Jews believed was through keeping the law. The lawyer likely expected an answer related to the law, and Jesus' response undoubtedly caught him by surprise.

Jesus responded with a question asking the lawyer what was written in the law and how did he understand it. The lawyer answered correctly by combining Deuteronomy 6:5 and Leviticus 19:18. To "love God, and love one's neighbor" captures the essence of the Ten Commandments. The first five give requirements for vertical relationships with God, and the other five give requirements for horizontal relationships with other people (Exodus 20:1–17). It was never God's intent for people to religiously follow a set of rules. He wanted people to honor him and care about others because of love. Love—not obligation—was the motivational force for observing the law. The lawyer got it right, and Jesus commended him.

The lawyer loved God, or at least he thought he did, but he had a problem with "neighbor." Under Roman rule, Israel had experienced a huge influx of non-Jews into the land. *What if a Gentile is my neighbor?* he thought, so he asked, "Who is my neighbor?" Jesus responded with the parable of the Good Samaritan.

A Traveler, a Priest, a Levite, and a Samaritan

The traveler—A man traveling from Jerusalem to Jericho was attacked by robbers. I've been on the Jericho Road. It has enough twists and turns to make a seasoned traveler sick. In Jesus' time you would take the Jericho Road at your own risk. The distance from Jerusalem to Jericho is approximately seventeen miles, but the elevation drops from 3,300 feet to below sea level with blind turns and high cliffs. The topography made it ideal for setting an ambush. It was infamous for robbery, yet many risked the danger because it was the shortest route from Jerusalem to Jericho. Though people usually traveled in groups, this man was traveling alone, which made him an easy target for bandits. He was ambushed, stripped of his clothes, beaten, and left for dead.

The priest—Though they served in the temple in Jerusalem, many of the priests lived in towns a short distance from Jerusalem. There were twenty-four units of priests, and each group served two separate weeks annually, which made it possible for them to live in towns other than the crowded city of Jerusalem. The priest was possibly returning home after serving in the temple for his assigned time. When the priest saw the wounded man, he didn't even continue on the same side of the road; instead, he crossed to the other side. It's possible the priest wanted to avoid ritual contamination by touching blood, but it seems more likely he was simply indifferent to the wounded man.

The Levite—The Levites were descendants of Levi and had been charged with assisting the priests in temple worship. When he saw the wounded man, he approached him; but was unwilling to help. He too crossed to the other side of the road.

Years ago, I was on a ministry trip with two other men in Kazakhstan. One afternoon we decided to visit the market in Almaty, the capital of Kazakhstan. A man approached us and tried to lure us out of the market with money. We didn't fall for his ruse. Later we found out that a gang used money to lure Westerners into a secluded place where they were beaten, robbed, and even stripped of their clothes. Their latest victim was in the hospital. Perhaps the Levite thought the wounded man was a decoy and that the robbers were hiding, waiting to ambush their next victim. We don't know why the Levite didn't help, only that he didn't.

The Samaritan—A despised Samaritan is the hero in the story. He uses oil and wine to treat the wounded man. He bandaged his wounds, possibly using strips of cloth torn from his white robe, which Samaritans customarily wore. He put the wounded traveler on his donkey and took him to a nearby inn. The next day he paid the innkeeper for additional lodging and offered to pay more if needed on his next trip. Most Jews would have found this story offensive.

To say that Jews and Samaritans didn't like one another would be an understatement. They hated each other. That doesn't mean all Jews and Samaritans hated one another, but the animosity between the two groups was centuries old. When the Assyrians overran Israel or the Northern Kingdom in 722 BC, they repopulated the area with Gentiles. The remaining Jews married with people from other nations and assimilated some of their religious beliefs. They were called Samaritans because the capital of Israel had been Samaria. The division between Jews and Samaritans intensified over the centuries. The Samaritans developed their own version of the Scriptures called the Samaritan Pentateuch, and built their own temple on Mount Gerizim. During the years between the testaments, the Jewish king John Hyrcanus destroyed their temple in 128 BC. It was rebuilt during the Roman period with help from Herod the Great. In some ways, the Samaritans' expectations for the Messiah were more accurate than those of the Jews. In Jesus' encounter with the Samaritans through his conversation with the woman at the well, the Samaritans concluded that Jesus was the Savior of the world—a belief that was not held by most pious Jews (John 4:42). In inaugurating the kingdom, Jesus ignored ethnic and cultural barriers. He had previously engaged a Samaritan woman in a conversation by asking her for a drink (John 4:1–42). And now he makes a Samaritan the hero in the parable, a feature that would have been highly offensive to most Jews.

Jesus' Question and the Lawyer's Answer

Jesus forces the lawyer to answer his own question by concluding with a question: "Which of these three do you think was neighbor to the man who fell into the hands of robbers?" (Luke 10:36).

I don't think the lawyer wanted to admit that it was the Samaritan, but he had no choice. He answered, "The one who had mercy on him" (Luke 10:37). Though he answered Jesus' question, he refused to say "the Samaritan."

Jesus didn't say, "Anyone who needs help is your neighbor," but challenged him to show that he truly believed what Jesus had taught by doing something. Jesus told him, "Go and do likewise" (Luke 10:37). We don't know how the Jewish lawyer responded, but Jesus' command either infuriated him or humbled him. Jesus was essentially saying, "Go and be a Samaritan—a good Samaritan." Ouch!

"Inclusion" and "Reversal"

The parable of the good Samaritan is about more than identifying a neighbor. It highlights two of the major themes in the Gospel of Luke— "inclusion" and "reversal." Luke gives more attention to Jesus' inclusive ministry than the other Gospels. He highlights Jesus' ministry to the poor, sinners, and women. In describing the ministry of John the Baptist, Luke quoted Isaiah 40:35 (Luke 3:4–6). The last verse identifies the inclusive scope of the Messiah's ministry: "And all people will see God's salvation" (Luke 3:6). The literal term for *people* is "flesh," which stresses all of humanity without any racial distinction. Luke records Jesus' healing of a centurion's servant, and commended him for his remarkable faith (Luke 7:1–10). The three parables in Luke 15 are in response to Jesus associating with tax collectors and sinners (Luke 15:1–2). Only Luke identifies the women who supported Jesus in his ministry (Luke 8:1–3).

The theme of "reversal" is a significant feature of many of Jesus' parables. "Insiders"—the rich, the religious, and the powerful— are excluded from the kingdom, and "outsiders"—the poor, the despised, and the humble—enjoy the blessings of the kingdom. The parable of the narrow door, for example, concludes with a statement of both inclusion and reversal (Luke 13:28–30): "There will be weeping and gnashing of teeth, when you see Abraham, Isaac and Jacob and all the prophets in the kingdom of God, but you yourselves are thrown out. People will come from east and west and north and south, and will take their places at the feast of the kingdom of God. Indeed there are those who are last who will be first, and first who will be last."

The parable of the good Samaritan answers the criticism and question of the Pharisees when Jesus and his disciples ate with tax collectors and sinners at Matthew's house. They asked Jesus' disciples, "Why does your teacher eat with tax collectors and sinners?" (Matthew 9:11). When Jesus heard their criticism, he said that it is not the healthy but the sick who need a doctor. And then told them they needed to learn what the Scriptures mean. "I desire mercy, not sacrifice" (Matthew 9:13). The priest and the Levite needed to learn that lesson as well.

IIIIIIIIIIIIIIIIIIIIIIIIIIIIIIIIII **REFLECT** IIIIIIIIIIIIIIIIIIIIIIIIIIIIIIIIII

1. How does the parable support Luke's emphasis on reversal? What are some contemporary examples of reversal in salvation?
2. How would you answer the question, "Who is my neighbor?"
3. Can you describe an experience where you had an opportunity to be a Good Samaritan?
4. Why is a willingness to help others an essential part of our witness for Christ?
5. How has this parable helped you to better understand the difference between religion and authentic faith?
6. Read Hosea 6:6 and Matthew 12:1–8. How do these verses emphasize that knowing God is more than religious ritual? What can we do to keep our walk with Christ from becoming merely a religious routine?
7. Read Revelation 7:9–10. How does this parable complement John's vision of a great multitude from "every nation, tribe, people and language" praising God in heaven?
8. Is there a group of people in your community like the wounded traveler? How can you be a Good Samaritan to them?
9. What new truth have you learned from this parable about the character of God? What can you do to develop this divine attribute in your life?

############################ **Memory Verse** ############################

But go and learn what this means: "I desire mercy, not sacrifice."
For I have not come to call the righteous, but sinners.

Matthew 9:13

Prayer

The Helpless Widow and the Unjust Judge

Luke 18:1–8

AUTHOR'S TAKEAWAY: *If we ever lose our sense of shame, there is no limit to the evil we might do.*—ADAPTED FROM KARL MENNINGER, *WHATEVER BECAME OF SIN?*

I am a very active person, and I love to workout, especially if I'm training for a race. I compete in triathlons, which include swimming, cycling, and running. On numerous occasions my friends have asked, "Why do you exercise so much?" My answer is usually because I don't want to drown in a race. Why am I disciplined to train? I do it so I can compete.

Several years ago when I was studying the life of Christ, I discovered a section in the Gospel of Mark that gives a snapshot of a day in the life of Jesus. In 1:21–39, Mark records Jesus' activities from sunrise to sunrise. It was the Sabbath, and in the morning Jesus taught in the synagogue at Capernaum. When confronted by a demon-possessed man, he delivered the man from the evil and unclean spirit. When he left the synagogue, Jesus went to the home of Simon (Peter) and Andrew, where he healed Peter's mother-in-law. He stayed there for the day (and watched football), but continued to minister in the evening. He healed people of multiple diseases and delivered others from demon possession. It was a long day, from sunrise until late in the evening. What did Jesus do the next morning? Did he sleep in? Nope! He rose early in the morning and went to a private place to pray (Mark 1:35). What this tells me is that Jesus' ministry was empowered by prayer.

Just as I train to compete, I need to pray to serve Christ. If Jesus fueled his ministry with prayer, how much more do we need to pray daily for power to serve our Savior. In the parable of the persistent widow and the unjust judge, Jesus contrasts the unwillingness of the judge to help the widow with the eagerness of God to hear our prayers.

Prayer

The parable of the persistent widow is the second of a triad of parables on prayer in the Gospel of Luke. The first is the story of the friend at midnight (Luke 11:5–8); the third is the parable of the Pharisee and the tax collector (Luke 18:9–14). This parable, which is found only in Luke, comes after Jesus' teaching about his second coming (Luke 17:20–27); so in addition to teaching about persistence in prayer, Jesus also encourages faithfulness because of the paradoxical delay in his promised return (Luke 18:8).

Widows and Unjust Judges

Jesus introduced the parable with an encouragement to pray and not give up, which means he apparently recognized the difficulty of prayer.

To encourage the discipline of prayer, Jesus tells a story about an unjust judge and a vulnerable widow. The problem of unjust judges in Israel was not new. Seven hundred years earlier, Amos, the prophet shepherd from Tekoa, rebuked the rich: "They trample on the heads of the poor as on the dust of the ground and deny justice to the oppressed" (Amos 2:7). He lamented injustice in the courts: "There are those who oppress the innocent and take bribes and deprive the poor of justice in the courts" (Amos 5:12). And he called on Israel to repent: "Hate evil, love good; maintain justice in the courts. Perhaps the LORD Almighty will have mercy on the remnant of Joseph" (Amos 5:15). We could give the same job description to some judges today.

Jesus begins with the judge, who neither feared God nor respected men. Like judges today, he may have had a lifetime appointment and couldn't be removed from office. Drawing on his extensive background experience in the Middle East, Kenneth Bailey relates the description of the judge to the importance of "honor and shame" in the first century. He believes that the word *respect* should read "not ashamed of what people thought." He explains, "The problem with this judge is not a failure to 'respect' other people in the sense of respecting someone of learning or high position. Rather it is a case of his inability to sense the evil of his actions in the presence of the one who should make him ashamed. But the whole world can cry 'Shame!' and it will make no impression on him."[1] I told my wife that no one thinks like this anymore, and she said, "Not true!" She told me that when she or one of her brothers did something really bad (I'm sure most of the time it was one of her brothers), her mom would say, "You ought to be ashamed of yourself!" The judge was unjust because he had no sense of shame.

In Luke 18:3, Jesus describes a widow who was the victim of a dishonest creditor ("adversary," NIV; "enemy," NLT). In a culture that was dominated by men, widows were particularly vulnerable; but God himself was their defender. In the law, Moses warned that God will hear the cry of widows and punish those who exploit them (Exodus 22:22–24). And Isaiah, the prophet, urged rulers and people to champion the plight of orphans and widows. "Learn to do right; seek justice. Defend the oppressed. Take up the cause of the fatherless; plead the case of widows" (Isaiah 1:17).

A Persistent Widow

Jesus doesn't explain the widow's financial problem. She may have been trying to collect from someone who owed her money, or a greedy creditor may have been trying to extort money from her. Whatever her exact complaint, people would have immediately identified with a helpless widow pleading for justice.

When the judge refused to hear the woman's case (Luke 18:4), she refused to take no for an answer. She kept pleading with him, and Jesus says the judge finally gave in because of her persistence. Though the judge didn't care what people thought, the woman's persistence was driving him crazy, and he was afraid she would eventually wear him out. The verb literally means "to give someone a black eye" (NLT, n. 18:5). It's possible the judge was concerned the woman might physically attack him, but it's better to interpret it as a figure of speech. A contemporary expression would be *to browbeat*. The judge gives in because he can't stand the woman's constant pestering.

Opposites

At this point in the story, Jesus gives it a surprising twist. He applies the woman's persistence to prayer and contrasts God with the unjust judge (Luke 18:6–7). God is the exact opposite of the judge, who didn't care about his reputation or the helpless widow. The Lord is both faithful and just.

But what about persistence in prayer? Is Jesus teaching that we can leverage God to answer our prayers by persistence? I don't think so. God is not like the judge, who finally helps the widow because she keeps pestering him. God is a loving heavenly Father who is always listening and is eager to answer our prayers. Jesus says, "I tell you, he will see that they get justice, and quickly. However when the Son of Man comes, will he find faith on the earth?" (Luke 18:8). This, however, raises more questions. What about divine delays and unanswered prayer? Jesus applies the parable specifically to the cries of God's people for justice, so the promise for answered prayer is not for all kinds of requests. And the delay is related to the coming of the Son of Man, when the kingdom will come in all its fullness. The question then is whether or not we will persevere in faithful prayer as Jesus taught in the Lord's (disciples') Prayer, "your kingdom come, your will be done, on earth as it is in heaven" (Matthew 6:10).

The question of unanswered prayer is more difficult. When we pray, we should keep in mind the distinction between God's permissive and directive will. In his sovereignty and wisdom, God has chosen to grant some requests only if we faithfully pray (James 5:16–17). But even with sincere and persistent prayer, we cannot change God's sovereign plans and purposes. The challenge is that sometimes it is difficult to distinguish between the two.

Darrell Bock says that Luke 18:7 may be the most difficult in Luke.[2] The NIV and NLT attempt to clarify the meaning of the term *makrothumia* with the translation, "Will he keep putting them off?" The basic meaning of *makrothumia* is "patience," which may seem contradictory to verse 8: "I tell you, he will see that they get justice, and quickly." But the contradiction is partially resolved by the reference to the return of the Son of Man in verse 8. When Jesus returns, he will speedily vindicate the righteous. But because of the unexpected delay between Jesus' promise and his actual second coming, he encourages faithful prayer.[3] Peter explains the reason for the delay in Jesus' return: "The Lord is not slow in keeping his promise, as some understand slowness. Instead he is patient (*makrothumia*) with you, not wanting anyone to perish, but everyone to come to repentance" (2 Peter 3:9). The apostle John also encourages us to anticipate and pray for the Lord's return, "'Yes, I am coming soon.' Amen. Come, Lord Jesus" (Revelation 22:20).

It's my opinion that in reference to the second coming, Jesus encourages persistence in prayer. Because of the unexpected delay in his return, Jesus wants believers from one generation to the next to persevere in prayer. So persistence in prayer is not about repeatedly asking God for the same request, but praying faithfully until the Lord returns.

1. Read Luke 18:2 and Proverbs 1:7.
   a. What were the two reasons the judge refused to help the widow?
   b. What does it mean "to fear the Lord," and why is "fear of the Lord" important according to Proverbs 1:7?
   c. Do you think it matters what people think of us? Why or why not?
2. Read Luke 18:4–5. Why did the judge change his mind about helping the widow? Do you think he relented because of a change of character? Why or why not?
3. Read Luke 18:4–5; Luke 11:9–11; and Philippians 4:6–7. When have you prayed and not received the answer you expected, or no answer at all? What do you think we should do when we pray and do not get an answer or the answer we expected?
4. Read Luke 18:3. Who are some of the people in your community who need help (may have been treated unjustly)? What can be done to help them?
5. In the parable, the judge represents God, but he is the exact opposite of the corrupt judge. Complete the following chart by listing the differences between the judge and God.

Judge	God
Corrupt/Unjust	
Refused to help	

Judge	God
Relented because of the widow's persistent pleading/Afraid she will wear him out ("give him a black eye")	
Slow in responding to the widow's cry for justice	
A human judge (a man)	

6. Read Luke 18:8. Jesus applies the parable to prayer and faithfulness until the return of the Son of Man. What is your practice of prayer, and how do you persevere in the discipline of prayer?

OPTIONAL

1. What about persistence in prayer? When we pray and God doesn't seem to answer, do you think we should continue making the same request?

Memory Verse

Do not be anxious about anything, but in every situation, by prayer and petition, with thanksgiving, present your requests to God. And the peace of God, which transcends all understanding, will guard your hearts and your minds in Christ Jesus.

Philippians 4:6–7

The Pharisee
and the Tax Collector

Luke 18:9–14

AUTHOR'S TAKEAWAY: *Relationship is more important
than religion, especially when talking to God.*

The story of the Pharisee and the tax collector (Luke 18:9–14)
is the third of Jesus' parables on prayer recorded in the Gospel
of Luke. The other two are the friend at midnight (Luke 11:5–8)
and the persistent widow (Luke 18:1–8). These parables, which
are recorded only in Luke, are consistent with Jesus' emphasis
that he was a man of prayer. Though he was God's unique Son, it
was essential for Jesus to nurture his relationship with his Father
through prayer.

The parable of the friend at midnight and the persistent widow
emphasize God's willingness to respond to prayer in all kinds of
circumstances. The parable of the Pharisee and tax collector looks
at prayer from a human perspective, and shows how prayer is a
window into the heart of the worshiper.

The Temple—"A House of Prayer"

When Jesus drove the money changers out of the temple, he called the temple a house of prayer. "'It is written,' he said to them, 'My house will be called a house of prayer, but you are making it a den of robbers'" (Matthew 21:13). Corporate prayers were offered at 9:00 a.m. and 3:00 p.m., but individuals could pray at any time. Jesus tells a story about a Pharisee and a tax collector who came to the temple to pray.

The name *Pharisee* comes from a word meaning "to separate." The Pharisees were probably the descendants of "the Hasidim" (the pious ones), who resisted the efforts of Antiochus Epiphanes to force Greek culture on the Jews during the period between the testaments. They resisted by separating themselves from others and devoting themselves to strict obedience to hundreds of rules on the law. They were the largest and most influential religious group in Israel at the time of Jesus, and were generally condemned by Jesus as hypocrites. In my book *The World of Jesus*, I included a chapter on the religious groups during the time of Christ, titled "When Religion Gets Sick." That doesn't mean all Pharisees were corrupt. Some, like Nicodemus, had a genuine interest in knowing what was pleasing to God (John 3:1–12). But most Pharisees were more interested in following the rules of their religion than fostering a relationship with God.

Jesus' audience would not have been surprised that he told a story about a Pharisee praying in the temple. They may not even have been surprised by how the Pharisee prayed. What would have caught them off guard was the tax collector and his prayer. Unlike Pharisees who were respected, tax collectors were despised. The Romans had a convenient but corrupt system for collecting taxes. Instead of collecting taxes directly from the people, the Romans paid the highest bidder for the right to collect taxes. The "tax collectors" then made a profit by collecting more than needed to pay the Romans. The system was obviously conducive to greed and abuse, and tax collectors were generally considered dishonest. But in addition to corruption, tax collectors were considered collaborators with the Romans. A story about a repentant tax collector would have captured everyone's attention.

They Went to the Temple to Pray

Jesus does not tell us when a Pharisee and tax collector went to the temple to pray, but he tells us what and how they prayed. The contrast is remarkable. The Pharisee was arrogant and self-righteous. He prayed,

> God, I thank you that I am not like other people—robbers, evil-doers, adulterers—or even like this tax collector. I fast twice a week and give a tenth of all I get.
>
> Luke 18:11–12

It is obvious the Pharisee's prayer was totally self-centered. You have to wonder if he was addressing God or boasting to himself. He was thankful he was not a criminal, and bragged about doing more than the law required. Instead of fasting only on the Day of Atonement, he fasted twice a week and tithed on all of his income. But what stands out is his statement that he was not like the tax collector. Instead of using a divine standard, he compared himself to a despicable tax collector. His estimation of himself would have been vastly different if he had compared himself to God.

In contrast, the tax collector came humbly and seeking mercy. He stood at a distance with his head bowed and beat his breast as a sign of remorse. He prayed, "God, have mercy on me, a sinner" (Luke 18:13).

No one would have been surprised by the prayers of the two men. They would have expected a religious leader to recite his piety and a tax collector to confess his sins. What was surprising is that Jesus vindicated the tax collector. He said, "I tell you that this man, rather than the other, went home justified before God" (Luke 18:14).

Jesus introduced the parable by addressing those who were self-righteous and looked down on others. Jesus sees a person's standing with God differently. Those who are deemed right with God (justified) are not those who boast about how good they are but who recognize their own unworthiness. The Pharisee attempted to justify himself. The tax collector prayed for mercy. He was made right with God; the Pharisee was not.

In conclusion, Jesus emphasizes reversal, a prominent theme in Luke's Gospel: "For all those who exalt themselves will be humbled, and those who humble themselves will be exalted" (Luke 18:14). Humility is a foundational virtue in our relationship with God and others. The prophet Micah asks the question, "With what shall I come before the LORD and bow down before the exalted God?" (Micah 6:6). The Pharisee should have paid attention to Micah's answer. "He has shown you, O mortal, what is good. And what does the LORD require of you? To act justly and to love mercy and to walk humbly with your God" (Micah 6:8). Paul exhorted the Philippians, "Do nothing out of selfish ambition or vain conceit. Rather, in humility value others above yourselves, not looking out for your own interests but each of you to the interests of others" (Philippians 2:3–4). Can you imagine how different the Pharisee's prayer would have been if he had considered the tax collector better than himself?

A Saint and a Sinner

Though Jesus spoke the parable before the cross, and his listeners would not have connected the parable to his sacrificial death, the parable anticipates the Pauline concept of justification by faith. Looking back to the cross, Paul explains why Christ became an atoning sacrifice for sins past and present—"He did it to demonstrate his righteousness at the present time, so as to be just and the one who justifies those who have faith in Jesus" (Romans 3:26). The Pharisee foolishly trusted in his own goodness; the tax collector recognized he was a sinner and trusted God. As one commentator has aptly stated, "Before God, the tax collector was acquitted. The Pharisee was not. The one went home a saint, the other a sinner."[1]

It is impossible to overstate the importance of humility. In both the Old and New Testaments, the writers commend the humble and warn the proud. In Psalm 18:27, David sang, "You save the humble but bring low those whose eyes are haughty." Isaiah says that God honors the humble, "These are the ones I look on with favor; those who are humble and contrite in spirit, who tremble at my word" (Isaiah 66:2).

Throughout his life, Jesus exemplified humility and stressed the necessity of humility for his followers. He said, "Take my yoke upon you and learn from me, for I am gentle and humble in heart, and you will find rest for your souls" (Matthew 11:29). In his first sermon, Jesus stated, "Blessed are the meek, for they will inherit the earth" (Matthew 5:5; see also Psalm 37:11). Jesus anticipates when the Lord will rule over the whole earth, and promised the humble will rule with him. As he did in this parable, Jesus turned the conventional way of thinking about honor and shame upside down in the parable of the wedding banquet. He taught that those who exalt themselves will be humbled, and those who are humble will be exalted (Luke 14:7–11).

Paul taught that humility was the key to unity: "Be completely humble and gentle; be patient, bearing with one another in love" (Ephesians 4:2). To encourage humility Paul quotes from an early hymn about the humiliation and exaltation of Jesus Christ. Though he preexisted in all of the fullness of deity, Jesus willingly gave his divine rights to take on a human nature. He humbled himself, was obedient to God, and surrendered to the ignominious death on a cross. Because of his son's humiliation, God exalted him. He raised him from the dead and seated him at his right hand with honor and authority over all creation (Philippians 2:5–11). Peter urges all believers to clothe themselves with humility because

"God opposes the proud but shows favor to the humble" (1 Peter 5:5; see also Proverbs 3:34 and James 4:6).

A popular adage captures the necessity of humility:

The gate of heaven is so low,
  no one can enter it except on his knees.

REFLECT

1. If you heard a prayer like that of the Pharisee, what would you think about that person's relationship with God?

2. How are we (believers) sometimes like the Pharisees, who were more concerned about keeping rules than nurturing a genuine relationship with God?

3. Read Luke 13:1–5. How is the tax collector an example of what people must be willing to do to trust Christ as Savior?

4. Read 1 John 1:9–10. Is confession a part of your regular prayer life? Why is it important to include confession in our practice of prayer?

5. Read Micah 6:8. What does it mean in your daily life to walk humbly with God? How do you develop humility?

6. Read Matthew 23:1–4. Rules can be both helpful (positive) and detrimental (negative) for spiritual growth. What are some of the rules or expectations of your church that are both positive and negative in a dynamic relationship with God?

7. Read Luke 14:11 and 1 Corinthians 1:26–31. Can you describe a situation where a person's standing with God was completely reversed because they trusted Christ as Savior? How was your life changed because you became a believer?

8. Like many religions, the Jews had scheduled times for prayer. They prayed in the temple daily at 9 and 3, but also

could pray at any time. Do you think it is important to have a set time or times for prayer? Does your church have a scheduled time for prayer? Why or why not? How have you included prayer in your daily or weekly routine?

1. Skim Psalm 51. This is David's confession and plea for mercy after his sin with Bathsheba.
   a. How is the prayer of the Pharisee different from David's prayer?
   b. What are the similarities between the prayer of the tax collector and David's prayer?

||||||||||||||||||||||||||||||| **Memory Verse** |||||||||||||||||||||||||||||||

For all those who exalt themselves will be humbled, and those who humble themselves will be exalted.

Luke 14:11

The Friend at Midnight

Luke 11:5–11

AUTHOR'S TAKEAWAY: *Why not ask?*

I haven't had many visitors in the middle of the night, but I can identify with the man in the parable, who didn't want to get out of bed for a midnight visitor. I taught Bible for over thirty-five years at Moody Bible Institute, and one of the reasons I taught for so long is that I liked students and enjoyed spending time with them outside of the classroom. However, there were some days when I came home, the only thing I wanted to see was the garage door opening and closing behind me. I was exhausted and a midnight visitor would have been an unwanted nuisance.

The parable of the friend at midnight (Luke 11:5–8) is the first of three parables in the Gospel of Luke on prayer. The other two are the parable of the persistent widow (Luke 18:1–8) and the parable of the Pharisee and the tax collector (Luke 18:9–14). All three are unique to Luke and give different perspectives on prayer.

Jesus Prayed

Jesus was both God and man. He had all the rights of deity, but he chose to limit his authority and power in order to become a man. He was humble and submissive to the will of his Father. There is no aspect of his dual nature where his humanity is more on display than in prayer.

Jesus was a man of prayer, so it is not surprising that after watching Jesus pray, his disciples asked, "Lord, teach us to pray, just as John taught his disciples" (Luke 11:1). Apparently John was also a man of prayer.

Jesus responded with what we know as the Lord's Prayer (Luke 11:2–4; cf. Matthew 6:7–14). The new and most remarkable revelation is that Jesus says that we can now address God as *Father*. It is a simple prayer that includes honoring God as a gracious, forgiving, and compassionate heavenly Father, and trusting him for our physical and spiritual needs.

Jesus then used one story and two parabolic analogies to teach more about prayer (Luke 11:5–13). In the parable of the friend at midnight, Jesus used a bad example to teach a positive lesson about prayer (Luke 11:5–10). In the first parabolic analogy, Jesus encourages approaching God under any circumstances (Luke 11:9–10), and in the second, he contrasts the difference between a cruel prankster and a loving father (Luke 11:11–13).

A Midnight Visitor

The story seems straightforward and simple. A man had an unexpected guest arrive in the middle of the night. He didn't have bread (food) for the man, so he went to his friend (neighbor) to borrow bread. Since people went to bed shortly after sundown, his friend was sound asleep. Instead of answering the door, the man complained about the inconvenience of the late night visit. He called out from his bed, "Don't bother me. The door is already locked, and my children and I are in bed. I can't get up and give you anything" (Luke 11:7).

At this point in the parable, the response of the man's friend seems reasonable, but then the story takes a surprising twist. He does get up—but not because of his friendship; it was because of the man's "persistence" (Luke 11:8 NASB) or "shameless audacity" (NIV). The traditional translation of *anaideia* as "persistence" comes from the reference to "knocking" in verses 9 and 10. I've opted for a translation more consistent with the lexical meaning of the term. The standard Greek lexicon (dictionary) defines *anaideia* as "lack of sensitivity to what is proper, and carelessness about the good opinion of others, and it offers the following translations: *shameless, impertinence, impudence, ignoring of convention.*"[1] The lexicon bases its suggested meaning on the prominence of honor and shame in the Greco-Roman world. The NLT attempts to combine the ideas of persistence and shame with the paraphrase "shameless persistence" (v. 8).

The other question is deciding if the reference is to the man calling to his friend, or if it's to the man in bed. If it refers to the man attempting to borrow bread, then it refers to "shamelessness" in waking his neighbor in the middle of the night; if it refers to the sleepy man in bed, then it refers to his fear that he will suffer shame in the community if he does not help his neighbor.

After evaluating the multiple options, New Testament scholar Richard Longenecker comes to the following conclusion: "Personally, I lean toward applying the noun *anaideia* and the pronoun *autou* to the petitioner, but see that only as a means of directing attention to the man in bed who will deal with his friend's 'shamelessness' and vindicate it." His conclusion is that the story is about "honor and shame," and believes the emphasis is the honor of God. "This is consistent with the action of God who honors his own name when his people dishonor it."[2]

God's Goodness

Jesus applies the parable to audacity in prayer. He promises God will answer those who are bold enough to ask, "For everyone who asks receives; the one who seeks finds; and to the one who knocks, the door will be opened" (Luke 11:10). God is the exact opposite of the man who wouldn't get out of bed to help his friend. Because of his honor, God is eager to answer prayer and will not allow the petitioner *to be shamed* by refusing his request.

In the parabolic illustrations, Jesus gives two absurd contrasts to teach about the goodness of God (Luke 11:11–13). To give a trusting child a snake or scorpion would be a cruel and possibly dangerous prank. God would never give us anything that would harm us. For example, he gives the good gift of the Holy Spirit to those who ask. Luke, who emphasizes the ministry of the Spirit, has substituted Holy Spirit for "good gifts."

|||||||||||||||||||||||||||||||||||||| **REFLECT** ||||||||||||||||||||||||||||||||||||||

1. Read Luke 11:2. What does it mean to you that you can address God as *Father* in prayer?

2. Read Luke 11:7. How is God different from the man who wouldn't get out of bed to help his friend?

3. Read Philippians 4:4–7. Though Paul encourages us to pray about everything, what are some of the reasons God may not answer our prayers?

4. Read Luke 11:8. What should we do when God doesn't answer our prayers? Is "no" the same as not answering? Why or why not?

5. Read Luke 11:8–10. The NLT translates *anaideia* as "shameless audacity," and applies it to the petitioner, not the man in bed. This suggests that we should never be ashamed to bring any request before God. What are some of the reasons why we might be reluctant to pray?

6. Read Luke 11:9–11. How does the parable embolden you in the discipline of prayer, knowing that God has promised to give "good gifts" to those who are bold enough to ask?

7. Based on your study of this parable, how would you answer the question in the author's takeaway (pg. 161)?

(pg. 161)

############################### **OPTIONAL** ###############################

1. Do you favor the traditional translation of *anaideia* as "persistence," or as "shamelessness," as suggested in this study?
2. What are the differences in the meaning and application of the parable if *anaideia* is translated "persistence" or "shamelessness"?
3. Read Luke 11:2 and Ezekiel 36:22–23. What is the relationship between prayer and God's honor (his holy name)?

############################### **Memory Verse** ###############################

Therefore say to the Israelites, "This is what the Sovereign LORD says: It is not for your sake, people of Israel, that I am going to do these things, but for the sake of my holy name, which you have profaned among the nations where you have gone."

Ezekiel 36:22

The Workers in the Vineyard

Matthew 20:1–16

AUTHOR'S TAKEAWAY: *Don't be envious; be thankful!*

The parable of the workers is both intriguing and troubling (Matthew 20:1–16). It is intriguing because of the generosity of the employer; it is troubling because it seems to promote wage inequity in the labor market. Modern-day labor unions would never allow an employer to pay everyone the same for vastly different hours at work.

Now Hiring

It was harvest season, so the landowner went early in the morning to the local worker pool to hire day laborers. He hired some that morning, offering to pay them a denarius—the normal wage for a day laborer. Then he hired more workers at nine, noon, and three, and promised to pay them a fair wage. He returned to town at five and noticed men standing around. He asked them why they weren't working. They answered that no one had hired them. Though late in the day, the landowner hired them. When

166

the workday was over, the owner began paying those hired last, first. And he paid all the workers the same, even though some had worked much longer than those hired later. Those who were hired first and had worked all day complained that it was not fair to pay those who had only worked one hour the same as those who worked all day. The landowner didn't buy it! They had agreed on a wage at the start of the day, and he told the complainers it was his money and he could do with it what he wanted.

But That's Not Fair, or Is It?

We would agree that what the landowner did wasn't fair—that is, if the point of the story was about workers and wages. But the parable is about the kingdom of heaven (Matthew 20:1). It's about God's abundant grace. Everyone is welcome in the kingdom, and it's never too late to enter.

REFLECT

1. Read Ephesians 2:8–10. How does this parable illustrate Paul's emphasis on salvation by grace, not works?
2. Read Matthew 25:14–30 and Luke 19:12–27. How would you explain the apparent contradiction between this parable and the parable about those individuals who were rewarded for multiplying the money (gold) they were given?
3. Read Matthew 20:11–12.
   a. What are the parallels between workers in this parable and the elder and younger brothers in the parable of the prodigal son? (See Luke 15:11–32.)
   b. What are the dangers of resentment, and how can we avoid it?
   c. What is the point in the parable about God's generosity?

4. Read Matthew 20:2–7 and Romans 3:23–24; 4:4–5. What does the hiring of workers at different times and paying them all the same wage imply about entrance into the kingdom of God?

5. How does this parable reinforce the truth that all people are of equal value, and that all who respond to God's gracious invitation will be accepted into the kingdom?

6. How would you use this parable to assure a person who thinks they are not worthy to be saved that they matter to God?

7. How would this parable help in counseling an older person that even though they might be near the end of life, God does not discriminate against anyone because of age?

OPTIONAL

1. Read 2 Corinthians 5:10. Do you think this parable condones believers who do nothing to serve God? Will they receive the same rewards as those who faithfully serve Christ? Why or why not?

Memory Verse

The grace of our Lord was poured out on me abundantly, along with the faith and love that are in Christ Jesus.

1 Timothy 1:14

The Lost Sheep
and the Lost Coin

Luke 15:1–10

AUTHOR'S TAKEAWAY: *Love is more important than the wedding ring.*

Many, many years ago when I was attending seminary in Denver, we lived on campus in one of the seminary's apartments. It was a small two-bedroom apartment, but it was adequate and affordable for our young family. One day, my wife said she couldn't find her wedding ring. I said that's okay, I was sure we'd find it. I was wrong. We searched everywhere and even vacuumed the carpet. No ring! I then said, "I'm sure we will find it when we move because we'll have to take out all the furniture and clean the apartment." I was wrong again. We never did find that ring. Well, Linda and I are still married fifty-plus years later, and I bought her another ring. Our experience is the opposite of the woman who lost a coin. Angels rejoiced when the woman found the coin; no angels rejoiced over my wife's lost ring.

The three parables in Luke 15 should be read together. All three are Jesus' response to the complaint by Israel's religious elite that he associated with people they despised.

> Now the tax collectors and sinners were all gathering around to hear Jesus. But the Pharisees and teachers of the law muttered, "This man welcomes sinners and eats with them" (Luke 15:1–2).

Though all three are about finding what was lost, each highlights a different aspect of God's amazing love. Because the parables of the lost sheep and the lost coin are short, they are included in this study. The parable of the prodigal son is in a separate study.

A Shepherd and His Sheep (Luke 15:3–7)

The area where I now live is ranch country. Modern-day cowboys and cows are part of the culture. In first-century Palestine, shepherds and sheep were a familiar part of their culture. Shepherds had been prominent in Jewish life for centuries. David was a shepherd, and many of the psalms reflect his experiences as a shepherd. He begins Psalm 23 with the imagery of a shepherd: "The LORD is my shepherd." The prophets often compared God to a shepherd. For example, Isaiah describes God as a compassionate shepherd: "He tends his flock like a shepherd: He gathers the lambs in his arms and carries them close to his heart; he gently leads those that have young" (Isaiah 40:11). Matthew continues the shepherd theme by combining Malachi 5:2 and 4 to identify the birthplace of the Messiah. "But you, Bethlehem, in the land of Judah, are by no means least among the rulers of Judah; for out of you will come a ruler who will shepherd my people Israel" (Matthew 2:6).

The Divine Shepherd

Two passages, Ezekiel 34 from the Old Testament and John 10 from the New, give us an insightful perspective on the parable of the lost sheep. Ezekiel assures Jews living in exile that when the Sovereign Lord returns, he will rescue his people from false shepherds who prey on the flock. God himself will shepherd his people, and set over them one shepherd who will gather the scattered sheep and lead them to green pastures (Ezekiel 34:1–24). In the New Testament, the passage in Ezekiel 34 provides the background for Jesus' "Good Shepherd Discourse" in John 10. Jesus, "the Good Shepherd," courageously protects his sheep and compassionately cares for them. He knows his sheep and they know him. The Good Shepherd is not cowardly. He does not run away when his flock is threatened by predators; he willingly sacrifices his life to protect them. And in a theologically significant statement, Jesus says he has complete control over life and death. "The reason the Father loves me is that I lay down my life—only to take it up again. No one takes it from me, but I lay it down of my own accord. I have authority to lay it down and authority to take it up again. This command I received from my Father" (John 10:17–18).

The Human Shepherd

In response to the criticism about his eating with "riffraff" (tax collectors and sinners), Jesus compares himself to a shepherd. The shepherd's flock is sizable: one hundred. He loses one. What does he do? He leaves the ninety-nine to search for the one lost sheep. Some commentators think that he did not put the other sheep at risk because there were other shepherds, or he put them in a pen. Either of those explanations is plausible, but Jesus doesn't say that's what the shepherd did. The focus of the parable is obviously on the one lost sheep. The shepherd may not have put the ninety-nine at risk, but he did leave them to search for the one. When I taught Bible survey to two mega-sections of two hundred students, I would leave the podium and look intently at the class, and then say, "Mary is missing. I have to find her." I would then walk out of the classroom and leave behind a bewildered group of students. I didn't leave the classroom for long or, like a bunch of sheep, students would begin to stray. When I returned, I said, "That's what the shepherd did to find one lost sheep."

When the shepherd found the sheep, he was so grateful he carried the sheep home. The lost sheep was probably so frightened and disoriented that the best way to get it home was to carry it. Once back in the village, the shepherd summoned friends and neighbors to celebrate with him.

To Seek and Save the Lost

Jesus concludes with the main point of the parable: "In the same way there will be more rejoicing in heaven over one sinner who repents than over ninety-nine righteous persons who do not need to repent" (Luke 15:7). Some think it is problematic that Jesus compares people to sheep because sheep do not repent, but repentance is not the point of the parable. Neither is Jesus comparing the religious leaders to the righteous. In chapter 16, he rebukes the Pharisees for greed and hypocrisy, and warns them that God knows their hearts. What they value, God hates (Luke 16:14–15). The main point is that Jesus came "to seek and save the lost" (Luke 19:10). And that's the reason he hangs out with riffraff. He is doing what God would do—recklessly seeking the lost. God loves those who are lost, and all heaven (God) rejoices when they are found.

|||||||||||||||||||||||||||||||||||||||| **REFLECT** ||||||||||||||||||||||||||||||||||||||||

1. Read John 3:16. How is this parable an illustration of John 3:16?

2. To what extent are you and your church willing to take a risk and perhaps be criticized for attempting to reach the lost?

3. Read Luke 15:1–2. Why do you think that even today, Christians sometimes criticize churches for aggressively seeking the lost? Is such criticism justified? Why or why not?

4. Do you think Jesus is using hyperbole (exaggeration) when he says that all heaven rejoices over one lost sinner who

repents, or is there actually joy in heaven? Why or why not?

5. Read 2 Corinthians 5:18–21. How does the imagery Paul uses in this passage supplement the main point in the parable of the lost sheep?

6. Read Acts 20:28–32. How are Paul's instructions to the Ephesian elders similar to the parable of the lost sheep?

7. In the parable, the shepherd searches for the lost sheep. How does this point in the parable distinguish Christianity from other world religions?

The Lost Coin (Luke 15:8-10)

Not a Shepherd but a Woman

With a few differences in the storyline, the parable of the lost sheep and the lost coin make the same point. In contrast to the woman who searches for a lost coin, the shepherd is a man. The shepherd leaves behind ninety-nine sheep to find one lost sheep, possibly putting the ninety-nine at risk; to search for the lost coin, the woman does not put the nine at risk. The shepherd searches for the lost sheep without any special equipment; the woman uses a lamp and a broom. Both the sheep and the coin are passive in the story. These and other details are interesting, but do not have any special meaning. Jesus' purpose is to refute the objections of the Pharisees and scribes about his eating with those they despised. In contrast to their hypocritical and harsh condemnation of sinners, Jesus emphasizes the love of God for the lost.

A Lost Coin

The parable is straightforward, though the actions of the woman might be considered somewhat ridiculous. A woman had ten silver coins, and she lost one. The Greek text identifies the coins as *drachmas*. A drachma was the wage for a day worker. It would not be of much value in today's currency, but it was perhaps important to the woman for her livelihood. Or it might have been part of her dowry, in which case it might have been somewhat equivalent to the wedding ring my wife lost.

Using a lamp and a broom, she searches diligently until she finds it. As in the parable of the lost sheep, she invites her friends and neighbors to rejoice with her. Jesus concludes with the point of application. "In the same way, I tell you, there is rejoicing in the presence of the angels of God over one sinner who repents" (Luke 15:10). The reference to "angels of God" is an indirect way of showing a high regard for God and avoiding offending Jews who were reluctant to use God's name.

Even the angels rejoice when one sinner repents. In *Interpreting the Parables*, Craig Blomberg suggests a third point in addition to the diligent search and rejoicing in recovering what was lost. He writes, "Just as the existence of the ninety-nine sheep and nine coins afford no excuse for not searching for what is lost, those who profess to be God's people can never be satisfied that their numbers are sufficiently great so as to stop trying to save more."[1]

||||||||||||||||||||||||||||||||||| **REFLECT** |||||||||||||||||||||||||||||||||||||||

1. What aspect of God's love is emphasized in the search for the lost coin?
2. What kind of object could you use in a story today that would make the same point as the parable of the lost coin?
3. How does this parable challenge us to make the lost a priority in our lives and the mission of the church?
4. How can we balance witness and worship in the mission of the church?
5. What is the point about the value of people in the woman's diligent effort to find a coin of modest value?

6. What new truths did you learn from the parables of the lost sheep and the lost coin? How will this affect your life as a Christ follower?

‖‖‖‖‖‖‖‖‖‖‖‖‖‖‖‖‖‖‖‖‖‖‖‖ **Memory Verse** ‖‖‖‖‖‖‖‖‖‖‖‖‖‖‖‖‖‖‖‖‖‖‖‖‖‖

But let the godly rejoice
Let them be glad in God's presence.
Let them be filled with joy.

Psalm 68:3 NLT

The Prodigal Son/ the Loving Father

Luke 15:11–31

AUTHOR'S TAKEAWAY: *The "Welcome Home" sign is on the door; why not come home?*

Except for messages on Jesus' birth at Christmas and his resurrection at Easter, I have heard more messages on the parable of the prodigal son than any other. At the church I attended for years in the Chicago area, the story of the prodigal son was central to the church's ministry. I did not grow up in a Christian home, but I was never what you would call a prodigal son; however, many men and women can readily identify with the younger son. And they are eternally grateful that God, like the loving father, welcomed them home.

"A Gospel within the Gospel"

The story of the prodigal son is the third parable in Jesus' response to the Pharisees' criticism of his welcoming tax collectors and sinners. Though the parables of the lost sheep, the lost coin, and the prodigal son all focus on God's love for the lost in contrast to the

Pharisees' condemnation of people they despised, each portrays a different perspective on God's grace. The parables of the lost sheep and the lost coin are about animals and property; the parable of the prodigal son is about people. The first two describe joy in heaven for the recovery of what was lost. In the third, the celebration takes place on earth. A third person is introduced in the story of the prodigal son—the older brother. And as many have noted, though this parable has historically been called "the parable of the prodigal son," it perhaps should be called "the parable of the loving father."

Tax Collectors and Sinners

The parables in chapter 15 are part of Luke's larger narrative of Jesus' final journey to Jerusalem that began in 9:51. "As the time approached for him to be taken up to heaven, Jesus resolutely set out for Jerusalem." If Luke had not been a physician, I think he might have been a tour guide because of the travel itineraries he gives us in the third Gospel and the book of Acts.

In his journey to Jerusalem, Jesus focused on teaching about the cost of discipleship and God's inclusive love for "outsiders"—those despised by the religious elite. Most of his teaching was in the form of parables. From 9:51 to 19:28, Jesus taught seventeen parables. Why parables? He used parables to challenge traditional thinking about "sinners," and to persuade people to think more inclusively about God's compassion and mission to "the lost."

It was predictable that most scribes and Pharisees would find Jesus' lifestyle and teaching offensive. Because Jesus allowed tax collectors and sinners to gather around him and listen to his teaching, the Pharisees and scribes (teachers of the law) muttered/grumbled, "This man welcomes sinners and eats with them" (Luke 15:2). Eating with someone meant more than today; it signaled total acceptance. This was as horrifying as inviting a street person into your home for dinner.

Jesus responded with the parables of the lost sheep, the lost coin, and the (lost) prodigal son.

There are no structural markers for dividing the parable of the prodigal son into three parts, but because of its length, I have divided it into three scenes: 1) the rebel son (vv. 11–16); 2) the repentant son (vv. 17–24); and 3) the older brother (vv. 25–32).

The Real Hero

The rebel son

The first scene focuses on the younger of the man's two sons. Showing utter disrespect for his father, the son demands (doesn't ask for) his share of the family inheritance. According to the law, the older of two sons should receive double (two-thirds) the inheritance as the younger (one-third). Since he wouldn't have normally received his share of the family inheritance until the death of his father, the younger son's request is unbelievably cruel. He is in effect saying, "I wish you were dead." Instead of protesting, the father grants his request. Every parent has probably faced a similar dilemma. Your son or daughter makes a decision that you know is not right, but you let them do it, hoping they will learn for themselves the consequences of bad choices.

It doesn't take long for the young man to realize he's made a terrible mistake. He squandered his inheritance in a "distant country," probably a Gentile territory. His circumstances were made worse by a famine. To survive, he was forced to work as a day laborer. His job is feeding pigs—animals considered unclean by Jews—so in addition to economic poverty, he is rendered ritually unclean. He is so hungry, he longs to eat the bean pods that were food for the pigs, but no one will give him anything. Now he is the one who is good as dead. His situation would be somewhat analogous to the homeless who sleep on the street and beg daily for food.

The repentant son

Though Jesus does not mention repentance, the prodigal is broken and contrite. The statement, "When he came to his senses," indicates a change of mind and probably a change of heart. On considering his circumstances, he concludes his father's hired servants are better off. At least they are not starving. He prepares a speech of reconciliation, and returns to his father. His confession is notable because he acknowledges he has sinned against heaven (God) and his father.

The prodigal didn't know what to expect. I'm sure he didn't anticipate what happened. Instead of disowning his son who had disowned him, the father was filled with compassion. He ran to meet his son while he was still a long way off, threw his arms around him, and kissed him. The father's undignified actions would have been shocking in an honor-shame culture. The prodigal attempts to give his rehearsed speech, but his father cuts him off. To restore him into the family, he orders his servants to bring the best robe, and put the family signet ring on his finger and sandals on his feet. These items were all tangible evidence of love and forgiveness. And he tells his servants to prepare a feast. (I can't help but recall this corny joke: Who, besides the elder brother, was not happy with the return of the prodigal son? The fatted calf, of course!)

The father's reason for the rejoicing is the first of two identical statements with important theological meaning. "For this son of mine was dead and is alive again; he was lost and is found" (Luke 15:24). The prodigal son was not physically dead, but he was spiritually dead, as are all men and women who are in rebellion against God, their heavenly Father. That's the bad news. The good news is that God's grace and love are greater than the wickedness of any prodigal. Paul said it best: "But because of his great love for us, God, who is rich in mercy, made us alive with Christ even when we were dead in transgressions—it is by grace you have been saved" (Ephesians 2:4–5).

179

The angry older brother

It's easy to get caught up in the story and forget that the parable is Jesus' response to criticism about his eating with people despised by the scribes and Pharisees. The elder brother represents Jesus' critics. He does not share his father's joy over his brother's return. When he found out the celebration was for his brother, he was so angry he wouldn't even go into the house. Like he did when the prodigal returned, the father went out to his older son and tried to reason with him. He complained that he had "slaved" (NLT) for years, and his father hadn't even given him a goat to celebrate with his friends. Even worse, he disowns his brother, calling him his father's son instead of his brother. "But when this son of yours who has squandered your property with prostitutes comes home, you kill the fatted calf" (Luke 15:30). The term *squandered* could also be translated "devoured." It's likely that the charge of prostitution is an exaggeration, but the implication is that his father has financed the prodigal's sinful lifestyle.

In spite of his elder son's hostility, the father is patient and kind. He addresses him as "my son," and assures him that he still has the right to the family inheritance. He again describes his younger son's miraculous transformation: "But we had to celebrate and be glad, because this brother of yours was dead and is now alive again; he was lost and is found" (Luke 15:32). In the Greek, verse 32 begins with *dei*, translated "we had" in the NIV. *Dei* is used frequently by Luke to indicate "divine necessity." As in the previous two parables, the recovery of what was lost is the occasion for a celebration because of the nature of God. He is the Father of amazing grace and infinite love, who will with open arms welcome home any prodigal! And what is the way home? It is through Jesus, who is "the way and the truth and the life" (John 14:6).

William Barclay concludes his devotional commentary on the prodigal son with this insightful statement about "the loving father": "For centuries the third parable has been called the Parable of the Prodigal Son. It would be far better if we were to call it the

Parable of the Loving Father for it is the father and not the son
who is the hero of the story."[1]

1. Read Luke 15:12. How would you respond to your child or
   a friend who was about to make a decision that you knew
   would plunge them into moral and/or economic ruin?
2. Read Luke 15:13–16. How are people today like the prodigal son? What do you think motivates people to indulge in
   a reckless and destructive lifestyle?
3. Read Luke 15:17–19. How do painful circumstances force
   us to reevaluate our choices?
4. Read Luke 15:20–24. What do the actions of the father
   imply about God's love and forgiveness? What would you
   say to a person who says they are so sinful God would
   never forgive them?
5. Read Luke 15:22–24. How does your church celebrate
   when sinners repent and trust Christ as their Savior and
   Lord?
6. Read Luke 15:28–30. Why do you think churches and individuals are sometimes like the older brother, and refuse
   to accept repentant sinners as part of God's family? How
   can we avoid resentment when we see people who we think
   are undeserving repent and trust Christ as Savior?
7. Read Luke 15:1–2. To what extent do you think we should
   associate with sinners? What are the benefits and risks of
   doing this?
8. How is the story of the prodigal son an encouragement to
   those who have ruined their lives by bad choices?
9. How is the response of the father an encouragement to
   people who have a prodigal son or daughter?

|||||||||||||||||||||||||||||||| **Memory Verse** ||||||||||||||||||||||||||||||||||

For God so loved the world that he gave his one and only Son, that whoever believes in him shall not perish but have eternal life.

John 3:16

The Unworthy Servant

Luke 17:7–10

AUTHOR'S TAKEAWAY: *There is no minimum wage in God's economy.*

Were the whole realm of nature mine,
That were an offering far too small;
Love so amazing, so divine,
Demands my soul, my life, my all.

Isaac Watts

Because of the horrible abuses of slavery in the past, we don't usually think of ourselves as slaves or servants. But that is exactly the analogy Jesus used when he wanted to emphasize the duty of discipleship.

What Is Expected?

Though the disciples didn't understand why, they reluctantly followed Jesus as he made his final journey to Jerusalem (Luke 9:51). Because Jesus knew his time was limited, he focused on preparing his followers for ministry in his absence. Though Jesus used an amazing variety of teaching methods, he primarily taught in parables on his way to Jerusalem, which Luke has recorded in his travel narrative (Luke 9:51–19:27). The parable of the obedient servant is one of numerous parables on what is expected of a loyal follower of Christ.

He Did What Was Expected

The story is about a master and a servant. The man was not wealthy. He had only one servant, who worked both in the fields and in the house. After the servant worked all day in the fields, he undoubtedly was tired and hungry, but he was still expected to prepare a meal for his master. The servant could eat only after the master was finished. The master doesn't even thank the servant. "And does the master thank the servant for doing what he was told to do? Of course not" (Luke 17:9 NLT).

Jesus then applies the parable to discipleship. He says that when we have done what is expected of us, we should say, "We are unworthy servants; we have only done our duty" (Luke 17:10).

God Doesn't Owe Us Anything

The point that the master doesn't even need to thank his servant seems harsh and ungrateful, but in first-century Greco-Roman culture, slaves were expected to serve their masters without complimentary encouragement. The disciples would have understood that this was not harsh. Plus, the term for *thank* is literally "grace" (*charis*). I would paraphrase the verse as follows: "Has the servant earned *the favor* (*charis*) of his master for doing what was expected?" The expected answer is "Of course not," as paraphrased in the NLT. Grace is not something we earn. It is undeserved and given freely by our gracious heavenly Father. However, in this case, disciples do not deserve grace for obediently serving Christ. In his explanation of this parable, Michael P. Knowles provides an insightful quote by John Calvin:

184

The object of this parable is to show that all the zeal manifested by us in discharging our duty does not put God under any obligation to us by any sort of merit; for as we are his property, so he on his part can owe us nothing.[1]

On a personal note, after attending seminary for three years, pastoring a church for four years, returning to seminary for two advanced degrees, and teaching the Bible for thirty-seven years, I retired. I didn't plan to do nothing and am grateful for the opportunity to write, but after I retired and slowed down a bit, I began experiencing the kind of physical issues that are inevitable with growing older and slower. When I complained, my wife said that the pains of growing old are better than the alternative. I asked her, "A better alternative than what?" She said, "Dying young." A good point, but not that helpful. I have sometimes thought, *After all my years of service for the Lord I don't deserve this!* But Isaac Watts, John Calvin, and Jesus remind me that God doesn't owe me anything; rather, I owe him everything.

The NIV and numerous other versions translate the term *achreios* as "unworthy." *Unworthy* does not mean or even imply *worthless*. Nothing that God created is worthless, and that includes us. As people created in his image, we are of great value to God. In fact, he created everything else to accommodate us.

But just because God doesn't owe us anything doesn't mean that he will not reward us. He will, but not out of obligation; rather, out of grace. The message is somewhat related to the parable of the workers in the vineyard. Though they all worked for different periods of time, they were all paid the same. From an employer-employee perspective, that was unfair, but not in God's economy, which is driven by grace, not merit.

REFLECT

1. What new truth did you learn from the parable about the grace of God? His sovereignty?

2. What do you feel God owes you? Has the parable changed your thinking? How?

3. What new truth have you learned that will motivate you in serving the Lord?

4. Read 1 Corinthians 3:5–9. How would you explain Paul's expectation that he and Apollos will be rewarded for serving Christ?

5. Do you think the concept of master-servant is beneficial for describing our relationship with Christ? If so, why? If not, why? What contemporary concept could we use to describe a similar relationship with Christ?

6. Read Ephesians 2:8–10. Why do you think Jesus emphasizes that we do not have any claim on God/Christ?

7. Read Colossians 1:23. How did Paul view his appointment to ministry? In what ways is God our master and we his servants?

8. Read John 15:9–17. What new relationship does Christ reveal in this passage? How is it similar and different from the master-slave relationship?

|||||||||||||||||||||||||||| **Memory Verse** ||||||||||||||||||||||||||||||||

But my life is worth nothing to me unless I use it for finishing the work assigned me by the Lord Jesus—the work of telling others the Good News about the wonderful grace of God.

Acts 20:24 NLT

The Sinful Woman and Two Debtors

Luke 7:41–43

AUTHOR'S TAKEAWAY: *PAID IN FULL. That's what Jesus has stamped on our debt to God!*

In this age of massive credit card debt, some credit card companies now offer debt forgiveness—not for all of the debt, but part of it if the debtor agrees to a payback plan. Most people would be thankful if part of their debt was forgiven; they would be overjoyed if all of their debt was canceled!

She Kissed Jesus' Feet

In the parable about debt forgiveness, the context is crucial for understanding what Jesus intended. Because Jesus had criticized the Pharisees for self-righteousness and discrimination against sinners, it is surprising that a Pharisee invited Jesus to dinner. For a formal dinner, guests would recline on couches with their feet extended behind them and eat from dishes placed on low tables.

It is also surprising that while Jesus was reclining at the dinner table, a sinful woman from the village slipped into the house and stood behind Jesus. She started weeping, wetting Jesus' feet with her tears, and wiping them with her hair. And then, what must have been even more shocking to the host, she kissed Jesus' feet and anointed them with expensive perfume (Luke 7:36–38).

The Pharisee didn't say anything, but he thought there was no way Jesus could have been a prophet because he would have known the woman was sinful and would not have allowed her to touch him.

Two Debtors

Jesus knew what Simon was thinking and challenged him with a short parable about two debtors (Luke 7:41–42).Like Nathan, the prophet, who used a parable to confront David after his sin with Bathsheba (2 Samuel 12:1–7), Jesus uses a parable to challenge Simon's prejudice toward people the Pharisees despised.

Jesus said, "Two people owed money to a certain moneylender." One owed a large amount: five hundred denarii. The other a small amount: fifty denarii. The lender forgave both debts. Jesus then asked Simon, "Now which of them will love him more?" Simon answered, "I suppose the one who had the bigger debt forgiven." Jesus commended Simon, "You have judged correctly." Simon's response, however, was lacking conviction. Perhaps he realized the parable was a clever setup.

The unnamed woman from the village was listening intently to the exchange between Jesus and Simon, yet she was undoubtedly surprised when Jesus looked directly at her and rebuked Simon. Unlike Simon, who did nothing to recognize Jesus as his guest, the woman washed Jesus' feet with her tears, honored Jesus with a kiss, and anointed him with expensive perfume. Speaking to Simon, Jesus said, "Therefore, I tell you, her many sins have been forgiven—as her great love has shown. But whoever has been for-given little loves little" (Luke 7:47). Then, turning to the woman, Jesus said, "Your sins are forgiven."

It's only now in the narrative that we discover Jesus was not the only guest. The other guests begin to murmur among themselves because Jesus has exercised divine authority by forgiving the woman's sins. But that's Luke's point. Jesus is not a mere man. He is God in the flesh and has come as the Savior of everyone, not merely the rich and religious elite.

To make certain that no one thinks salvation is by works, Jesus says to the woman, "Your faith has saved you; go in peace." In both his Gospel and the book of Acts, Luke highlights repentance as the anticipated response of genuine faith. And in this account, Luke shows how a sinful woman honored Jesus, not to earn salvation, but as a response of her faith and love for her Savior.

It is important to note how this passage is consistent with Luke's focus on Jesus' ministry to outsiders—the kind of people pious Jews despised. In this narrative, Luke emphasizes that Jesus was the Savior of everyone by contrasting the faith of a sinful woman with the ingratitude of a self-righteous Pharisee.

REFLECT

1. Read Luke 7:36. Why do you think Simon, a Pharisee, invited Jesus to dinner at his house, since most Pharisees were offended by Jesus? I think most would agree that rather than avoid people who have different opinions on certain issues, we might learn something if we talked to them. What are some of the ways we can engage people with different views in polite conversation?

2. Read Luke 7:36–38. What does the way Simon treated Jesus reveal about his attitude toward Jesus? In contrast, what do the woman's actions reveal about her attitude? How do our actions reveal how we view Jesus? What are some of the ways we can show love for Christ?

3. Read Luke 7:41–42. Why do you think Jesus told a parable rather than directly rebuking Simon for his lack of

hospitality? What are some of the advantages of telling a story (parable) to make a point in a potentially tense situation?

4. Read Luke 7:41–42, 48–50; Luke 24:45–49; and Acts 2:38. What do the actions of the moneylender reveal about the character of God? "To forgive" means "to cancel." What is the debt we owe to God, and what is the basis for forgiveness?

5. Read Luke 7:41–42. In thinking about how faith in Christ results in a miraculous transformation, do you think the following people would identify more with Simon or the unnamed woman? Why?

   a. Joshua 2:1–7

   b. First Samuel 3:19–4:1

   c. Acts 4:32–37

   d. Philippians 3:1–11

   Do you identify more with Simon or the woman? Why?

6. Read Ephesians 3:14–21. How does this story and parable motivate you to love the Lord?

|||||||||||||||||||||||||||||||||||||||| **OPTIONAL** ||||||||||||||||||||||||||||||||||||||||

1. Read Luke 8:1–3. How was Jesus' view of women different from most Jewish men in the first century? How has the account of the sinful woman affected your view of women?

2. Do you think it is always true that those who have been forgiven the most are the most grateful? Why or why not?

|||||||||||||||||||||||||||||||||| **Memory Verse** ||||||||||||||||||||||||||||||||||

And forgive us our debts,
   as we also have forgiven our debtors.

Matthew 6:12

The Wise and Foolish Builders

Matthew 7:24–27; Luke 6:47–49

AUTHOR'S TAKEAWAY: *If you don't have flood insurance, you should build your house on a rock-solid foundation.*

Storms are one of the most powerful forces of nature. Hurricanes and tornadoes can cause catastrophic damage to property and even loss of life. I survived two tornados—one in Texas and the other in Illinois. The one in Texas was the most terrifying. I was driving west and did not pay attention to the dark, threatening clouds gathering on the horizon. I drove directly into the path of the storm without realizing what was happening. Almost without warning, I was suddenly in total darkness with small objects flying across the highway. I didn't know if I should stop or keep driving. I chose to keep driving. I drove slowly with my lights and emergency flashers on. Fortunately, I was on the edge of what I later learned was a west Texas tornado, and within minutes drove out of the storm. It is not surprising that Jesus used a life-threatening storm to warn about a day of judgment.

191

Kingdom Righteousness

The parable of the two builders is included in both Matthew and Luke, and serves as a conclusion to Jesus' inaugural message on his expectations for authentic kingdom righteousness—a righteousness motivated by a desire to please God (Matthew 5–7:29; Luke 6:17–49). The message is commonly called the Sermon on the Mount because Matthew records that Jesus taught from a mountainside (Matthew 5:1). Luke's version is sometimes called the Sermon on the Plain because he records that Jesus spoke on a plain or level place (Luke 6:17). Though some believe Matthew and Luke record two different messages, I take the view that the two Gospels give a slightly different description of the same message. In both Gospels, Jesus describes a lifestyle that conforms to the righteousness of God in contrast to the pseudo-righteousness of the Pharisees (see Matthew 5:17–20).

After exposing the hypocritical righteousness of the Pharisees and describing kingdom righteousness, Jesus concludes with both a warning and a challenge. He warns that only those who profess to follow Jesus will be exposed in the day of judgment: "Not everyone who says to me, 'Lord, Lord,' will enter the kingdom of heaven, but only the one who does the will of my Father who is in heaven" (Matthew 7:21). In the parable of the two builders, Jesus appeals for a decision.

Foolish or Wise

Most everyone who grew up going to church will remember the children's song about the foolish and the wise men: The foolish man built his house on sand, and when the rains came down, the house washed away; the wise man built his on rock, and it stood firm against the torrential rains.

We have both a house and a cottage on a river in Colorado. We have insurance on the house but not on the cottage. Why on one and not the other? The cottage is on the flood plain of the river, so no one will insure it, while the house is on higher ground, and very insurable. In the story of the two builders, one is depicted as wise and the other as foolish. Both built houses on a flood plain. The wise builder prepared for the possibility of natural disaster by building his house on a foundation of rock. The other built on sand. He was foolish because he didn't anticipate what would happen if there was a catastrophic storm. When the river flooded, the house of the wise man withstood the storm; the house of the foolish man was swept away. By using the imagery of a powerful storm, Jesus gave a sense of urgency to his warning.

Jesus, James, and the Prophets

Though trained as a carpenter, Jesus wasn't giving a lecture on where and how to build a house. He was challenging his disciples to a radical kingdom lifestyle. The person who hears and obeys Jesus' words will survive in the day of judgment; the person who doesn't will not.

James gives the same warning using the imagery of a mirror. He says that if you hear God's word and do nothing, you are like a person who looks in a mirror and immediately forgets what he looks like (James 1:22–25).

Both Jesus and James were echoing the warning of the prophets. Jeremiah was shocked when he stood in the presence of the Lord and saw Israel's religious leaders from the Lord's perspective. Priests and prophets were ungodly and wicked. Instead of turning people away from sin, they encouraged wickedness and gave Israel false hopes. The prophet warned that the Lord's anger would burst on them like a destructive storm (Jeremiah 23:18–20). Using similar imagery, Ezekiel denounces false prophets:

> This will happen because these evil prophets deceive my people by saying, "All is peaceful" when there is no peace at all! It's as if these people have built a flimsy wall, and these prophets are trying to reinforce it by covering it with whitewash! Tell these whitewashers

that their wall will soon fall down. A heavy rainstorm will under-
mine it; great hailstones and mighty winds will knock it down.
And when the wall falls, the people will cry out. "What happened
to your whitewash?"

Ezekiel 13:10–12 NLT

Where Are You Building?

The application of this parable is threefold. First, Jesus doesn't tell
a story about a man who built a house and one who didn't. Why?
Because everyone is building a house. The house is your life. The
question is not whether to build or not, but on what foundation
are you building? To build your life on any other foundation than
Jesus is foolish. Your house will not stand in the day of judgment.
Who is wise? The person who hears the words of Jesus and obeys.
That person's house will survive the day of judgment. Paul warned
the Corinthians of the foolishness and futility of building on any
foundation other than Jesus Christ:

> Because of God's grace to me, I have laid the foundation like
> an expert builder. Now others are building on it. But whoever is
> building on this foundation must be very careful. For no one can
> lay any other foundation than the one we already have—Jesus
> Christ.

1 Corinthians 3:10–11 NLT

Second, though Jesus' primary purpose was to warn about
climatic judgment, the parable has implications for sustain-
ing us through unexpected crises in life. The two men built
the same house and experienced the same storm. The house of
the wise man was not protected from the storm, but it stood
because it was built on a solid foundation. The Lord has not
promised that believers will be protected from adversities in
life, but he has promised that we can survive the storms of life
knowing that God's grace is more than adequate to sustain us

194

in all circumstances. The apostle Paul ironically boasted about his suffering, even his "thorn in my flesh" (2 Corinthians 12:7). He begged the Lord to take it away, but instead discovered the paradox of power in weakness:

> Three times I pleaded with the Lord to take it away from me. But he said to me, "My grace is sufficient for you, for my power is made perfect in weakness." Therefore I will boast all the more gladly about my weakness, so that Christ's power may rest on me. That is why, for Christ's sake, I delight in weakness, in insults, in hardships, in persecutions, in difficulties. For when I am weak, then I am strong.
>
> 2 Corinthians 12:8–10

Third, to live as if this life was all that mattered is foolish. God is a loving Father, but he is also a just Judge. We will all stand before his divine court. Jesus repeats an implied warning in the parable of the wise and foolish bridesmaids (Matthew 25:1–13). Paul infuriated the philosophical agnostics at Athens when he claimed the resurrected Christ would judge them (Acts 17:29–31). He defended his apostleship against the charges of his opponents at Corinth by stating that no one but the Lord has the right to judge: "My conscience is clear, but that does not make me innocent. It is the Lord who judges me. Therefore judge nothing before the appointed time; wait until the Lord comes. He will bring to light what is hidden in darkness and will expose the motives of the heart. At that time each will receive their praise from God" (1 Corinthians 4:4–5; see also 2 Corinthians 5:10; 2 Timothy 4:2). The writer to the Hebrews argued for the once-and-for-all death of Christ by warning that after death comes judgment: "Just as people are destined to die once, and after that face judgment . . ." (Hebrews 9:27). John describes a court hearing in which the dead stand before the throne of God (Revelation 20:11–15). The parable of the two builders compels us all to ask the question, "Will my house stand in the day of judgment?"

1. Though the parable is about the material world, Jesus is certainly referring to the spiritual realm. What are some of the differences between a person who has built their life on a rock and one who has built on sand?

2. Read Psalm 7:10–13; 98:7–9. What does the psalmist mean when he says that God will judge the world in righteousness?

3. Read Revelation 20:11–15. To what extent do you think we should warn unbelievers about a day of judgment? How do we balance the message of God's love with a warning of judgment?

4. Read Romans 8:31–39. Though the parable is about final judgment, what are some of the storms of life? How does faith in Christ make a difference in how we respond to those storms?

5. Read 1 Corinthians 4:5. How are you living your life (building your house) so it will stand in the final judgment? Simply put, how are you preparing for eternity?

6. What changes will you make in your life as a result of studying this parable?

1. What contemporary parable could be used to warn people of final judgment?

Because of God's grace to me, I have laid the foundation like an expert builder. Now others are building on it. But whoever is building on this foundation must be very careful. For no one can lay any other foundation than the one we already have—Jesus Christ.

1 Corinthians 3:10–11 NLT

The Rich Fool

Luke 12:13–20

AUTHOR'S TAKEAWAY: *Life is not measured by how much you possess but by what you do with your "stuff."*

I have a friend who served with her husband as a missionary in Brazil for over thirty years. She is the daughter of a rancher who owned a huge ranch in Montana. While her father was living, he and her brother worked the ranch together; but when their father died, it was his intent that the ranch be divided between his children. As with many family squabbles, the situation was complicated by the brother's wife, who insisted on keeping the ranch for herself and her children. Whatever the exact reason, the brother refused to divide the ranch with his sisters. To her credit, my friend refused to take legal action against her brother. She was not foolish, and knew that honoring and serving God was far more important than material possessions.

Tell My Brother

Jesus told the story of the rich fool in response to a request by an unnamed man in the large crowd milling around him. Like my friend's brother, the man's brother refused to share his inheritance.

Since it was customary to ask a rabbi to settle a legal dispute, the man asked Jesus, "Teacher, tell my brother to divide the inheritance with me" (Luke 12:13).

Instead of honoring the man's request, Jesus warned about the danger of covetousness. Luke, who was a physician, was undoubtedly affluent, but he knew the dangers of greed. We know from the book of Acts that he was a traveling companion of the apostle Paul, and it is reasonable to assume that he sometimes used his personal resources to support their missionary work. Whether or not that was the case, in his Gospel, Luke repeatedly condemns the selfish accumulation of personal wealth. The parable of the rich fool is a classic example.

Don't Be Fooled

Jesus told a story about a farmer who had an unexpected and incredibly large harvest that would make him very rich. It was so abundant, he didn't have large enough barns to store the grain. It is unlikely that farmers today could become rich through farming; individuals are more likely to become wealthy through intangible things like technology, e.g., Microsoft, Apple, Facebook, Amazon, etc.

The accumulation of wealth is not inherently evil. In both the Old and New Testaments, wealthy men and women are honored for their faith and generosity—Abraham, Deborah, Solomon, Barnabas, Lydia, etc. What the Bible condemns is greed. Paul warns about the dangers of lust for money. "Those who want to get rich fall into temptation and a trap and into many foolish and harmful desires that plunge people into ruin and destruction. For the love of money is a root of all kinds of evil. Some people eager for money have wandered from the faith, and pierced themselves with many griefs" (1 Timothy 6:9–10).

The rich fool should have heeded Paul's warning. To store his abundant harvest, the farmer tore down his old barns and built bigger ones. Instead of using his wealth to advance God's kingdom, he made plans for a totally self-indulgent lifestyle. The repeated use of the personal pronoun "I" exposes his obsession with himself. He thought he could party for years, and said to himself, I will "eat, drink and be merry" (Luke 12:19). The problem wasn't his unexpected wealth but his godless intentions. In his plans, he completely excluded God.

Most modern-day investment counselors would have agreed with his decision to use his wealth for a hedonistic and self-indulgent lifestyle. But not God! He said, "You fool! You will die this very night. Then who will get everything you have worked for?" (Luke 12:20 NLT). The man either forgot or ignored the wisdom of his ancestors, who believed that the enjoyment of life was a gift from God. The writer of Ecclesiastes observed, "So I decided there is nothing better than to enjoy food and drink and to find satisfaction in work. Then I realized these pleasures are from the hand of God. For who can enjoy anything apart from him" (Ecclesiastes 2:24–25 NLT).

Jesus explained the point of the story when he said, "Yes, a person is a fool to store up earthly wealth but not have a rich relationship with God" (Luke 12:21, NLT). I heard one speaker explain with a bit of humor, "You can't take it with you. I've never seen a hearse pulling a U-Haul." He was right! Paul's advice to the rich is also an apt commentary on this parable.

> Teach those who are rich in this world not to be proud and not to trust in their money, which is so unreliable. Their trust should be in God who richly gives us all we need for our enjoyment. Tell them to use their money to do good. They should be rich in good works and generous to those in need, always being ready to share with others. By doing this they will be storing up their treasure as a good foundation for the future so that they may experience true life.
>
> 1 Timothy 6:17–19 NLT

It Really Isn't Our Money

I think we would all agree that we should use our resources to advance the kingdom of God and not squander them on selfish pleasures.

But what about saving for unexpected emergencies and retirement? Would you agree with Blomberg, who seems to argue against accumulating wealth for calamities and retirement? He quotes John Purdy, who contends that we should only work hard enough to provide for the necessities of life and leave the future in God's hands.[1]

I can agree somewhat with Blomberg, but I also see a tension between merely working for the necessities of life and accumulating wealth. Wealthy people can make generous contributions to the work of the kingdom. Poor people can't. It is significant that in 1 Timothy 6:17–19 Paul doesn't condemn the rich but urges them to use their wealth to help those in need. I think the issue is ultimately a matter of motives.

REFLECTIONS

1. What kind of story would Jesus tell today to warn about the evils of greed?

2. Read Luke 12:16–18. If you have expendable income at the end of the month, what do you think you should do with it? Save it, invest it, or give it away? Why?

3. Read 1 Corinthians 16:1–4. What are two guidelines Paul gives the Corinthians for giving? What guidelines do you use for your giving?

4. Read 2 Corinthians 8:1–7. Though most of us are probably not wealthy, why does Paul commend the Macedonian churches for their giving? What can we learn about giving from the Macedonian churches? Note: I have written a study on "grace giving" in *102 Fascinating Bible Studies*, explaining why the tithe is not required for New Testament believers!

5. Read 1 Timothy 6:6–10. What are some of the contemporary dangers of the lust for wealth? How can we avoid them?

6. If you were suddenly to become a multimillionaire, what would you do with your unexpected wealth?

7. To what extent should we plan for the future, including retirement? Should we save to provide an inheritance for our children? Why or why not?

8. Read 1 Kings 10:1–13.

   a. When the Queen of Sheba saw Solomon's kingdom, who did she credit for making him wealthy?

   b. Though Solomon was immensely wealthy, what were the other characteristics for which she commended Solomon?

   c. How can we use our resources, especially money, as a testimony of God's goodness?

9. How has the study of this parable influenced changes in your lifestyle and how you spend your money?

|||||||||||||||||||||||||||||||||| **Memory Verse** ||||||||||||||||||||||||||||||||||

Teach those who are rich in this world not to be proud and not to trust in their money, which is so unreliable. Their trust should be in God, who richly gives us all we need for our enjoyment.

1 Timothy 6:17 NLT

The Wicked Tenants

Matthew 21:33–46

Almost everyone who owns rental property has had the unfortunate problem of collecting rent from deadbeat tenants. There are laws governing such situations. We can impose late penalties or, in a worst-case scenario, we can evict them.

The Triumphant King

Jesus told a story about deadbeat tenants to warn Israel's religious leaders that God's patience is limited. The context for the story is the Passion Week—the week Jesus was crucified. The Passion Week began on Sunday when Jesus made a triumphal entry into Jerusalem. After a loud and enthusiastic welcome, Jesus went to the temple where he found that money changers and merchants had turned the temple into a bazaar. Jesus erupted in anger and drove them out. He spent Sunday night in Bethany, but returned to Jerusalem on Monday. While he was teaching in the temple courts, the chief priests and elders confronted him. "By what authority are you doing these things?" they asked. "And who gave you this authority?" (Matthew 21:23). Knowing their question was insincere, Jesus responded with a question about John's baptism that exposed the hardness of their hearts. They refused to answer and pleaded ignorance. Because they refused to answer, Jesus said, "Neither will I tell you by what authority I am doing these things" (Matthew 21:27). Jesus was not naïve. He knew they had already decided to kill him, and as Barclay comments, he went to his death "not like a hunted criminal, and not apologetically, but like a triumphant king."[1]

Deadbeat Tenants and the Beloved Son

The story of the wicked tenants is the second of a triad of parables that Jesus taught after the angry confrontation with the chief priests—two sons (Matthew 21:28–32), the wicked tenants (Matthew 21:33–46), and the wedding banquet (Matthew 22:1–14). The parable of the wicked tenants is found in all three Synoptic Gospels in the same context with the same meaning (Matthew 21:33–46; Mark 12:1–12; Luke 20:9–19). It was Jesus' parabolic warning to Israel's religious leaders who were determined to kill him.

The parable is historically plausible. Under Roman rule in the first century, absentee ownership in Israel was common. Rather than farm large tracts of land, the wealthy would lease it to tenants. The other important historical element is the imagery of a vineyard. In the Old Testament, Israel is often considered God's vineyard; most Jews would have immediately connected the nation to a vineyard.

Though we should not turn a parable into an allegory by creating meaning for all the details, it is important in this parable to identify the four primary characters. The owner of the vineyard is God. The tenants are Israel's religious leaders past and present. The servants are the prophets, and the son is Christ.

Two New Testament passages help in interpreting the parable. First, in his lament for Jerusalem, Jesus describes how the prophets were often mistreated, "Jerusalem, Jerusalem, you who kill the prophets and stone those sent to you, how often have I longed to gather your children together, as a hen gathers her chicks under her wings, and you were not willing. Look, your house is left to you desolate. For I tell you, you will not see me again until you say, 'Blessed is he who comes in the name of the Lord'" (Matthew 23:37–39). Manasseh, king of Judah, filled Jerusalem with the blood of God's servants. And according to Jewish history, he ordered Isaiah sawed in two. During the Babylonian siege of Jerusalem, Zedekiah ordered Jeremiah arrested. He was then thrown into a dry well and left to die. The parallel between the prophets and the servants is obvious.

Second, the writer to the Hebrews identifies the son as God's last spokesman. "In the past God spoke to our ancestors through the prophets at many times and in various ways, but in these last days he has spoken to us by his Son, whom he appointed heir of all things and through whom also he made the universe" (Hebrews 1:1–2). The son is obviously Jesus, whom both Mark and Luke identify as the owner's "beloved son" (Mark 12:6; Luke 20:13).

What Will He Do to Those Tenants

The plot of the parable is easy to follow. After a man planted a vineyard, he rented it to tenants and moved. At harvest time, he sent a servant to collect a share of the harvest. Instead of paying their rent, they beat the servant. Luke says this happened three times. Matthew says the owner sent multiple servants, who were beaten, killed, and stoned. Mark says the servants were beaten and sent away empty-handed, wounded and shamed, or killed. The tenants' treatment of the servants represents Israel's rejection of the prophets.

Finally, the owner decided to send his beloved son (Mark and Luke), who represents God sending his Son to Israel. He thought the tenants would respect him, but instead they plotted to kill him, thinking that they could claim the property if there was no heir, as was allowed by Jewish law. They were blinded by greed. Did they really think they could get away with murdering the owner's son? Jesus asks, "What will he do to those tenants?" (Matthew 21:40). He answers his own question, saying he will destroy those evil men and give the vineyards to others. Jesus warns that God will exchange Israel's corrupt leaders with others who would faithfully serve him. The "others" would include both Jews and Gentiles. Only Luke records the shocked response of the Jewish audience: "God forbid!" (20:16).

Reversal

Citing Psalm 118:22–23, Jesus reiterates the theme of reversal in the kingdom revolution. The stone rejected by the builders has become the cornerstone/capstone for the building. What the builders thought useless becomes the crucial stone for stabilizing the building. It is impossible to miss the application of the psalm to Jesus and the religious leaders.

In Matthew, Jesus connects the parable directly to the kingdom: "Therefore I tell you that the kingdom of God will be taken from you and given to a people who will produce its fruit" (21:43). And then he concludes with a warning about the devastating power of the stone (Son): "Anyone who falls on this stone will be broken to pieces; anyone on whom it falls will be crushed" (Matthew 21:44).

|||||||||||||||||||||||||||||||||||||| **REFLECT** ||||||||||||||||||||||||||||||||||||||

Kingdom Truths

1. Though the church is not the kingdom, how would the parable apply to the church in America?
2. Read Isaiah 5:1–7. How is this parable related to Isaiah's Song of the Vineyard?
3. Read Mark 12:6 and Luke 20:13. How do Mark and Luke describe the owner's son? What does this reveal about the

relationship between the Father and Son? See Luke 3:22 and 2 Peter 1:17. Why does this make the rejection of the son even more serious?

4. Read Matthew 21:42–44. How does Jesus' teaching about the stone from Psalm 118 support his death and exaltation (victory through suffering and death)?

5. Read Matthew 21:43; Mark 12:8; and Luke 20:16. What is Jesus' new revelation about the growth of the kingdom?

Personal Application

6. Read Acts 4:10–12 and Hebrews 1:1. How does the parable illustrate the message that Jesus is the only and last provision of salvation? Why do you think the religious leaders didn't recognize Jesus as God's Son and last provision for their salvation? What are some of the reasons why people today reject Jesus as the only Savior?

7. How does this parable motivate you in your stewardship of the kingdom?

8. Read 1 Timothy 1:16 and 2 Peter 3:8–9. How does the parable illustrate the patience of God? What is one example of God's patience in your life?

9. What new truths did you learn about God? How will what you learned affect how you live?

|||||||||||||||||||||||||||||||| **Memory Verse** ||||||||||||||||||||||||||||||||

While you were watching, a rock was cut out, but not by human hands. It struck the statue on its feet of iron and clay and smashed them. Then the iron, the clay, the bronze, the silver and the gold were all broken to pieces and became like chaff on a threshing floor in the summer. The wind swept them away without leaving a trace. But the rock that struck the statue became a huge mountain and filled the whole earth.

Daniel 2:34–35

The Barren Fig Tree

Luke 13:6–9

AUTHOR'S TAKEAWAY: *Uselessness invites disaster.*—WILLIAM BARCLAY

There is a premier spine surgeon in the area where I live who may have trained under Doctor Luke. I'm kidding, of course, but the two men are both physicians and have a common feature in their practice: Both emphasize repentance. However, the spine surgeon doesn't call it repentance. He is well-known and popular, and it's difficult to get an appointment to see him. And after an exam and tests, if you need surgery, there is no guarantee he will do it. He requires his patients to change their lifestyle (aka repent). For example, if a person is overweight, a smoker, or drinks excessively, he insists they make lifestyle changes before he does surgery. He asks those who are overweight to lose excessive pounds. If an overweight person says they can't lose excess pounds, he won't do surgery. They will need to find another physician.

I don't know if Luke did that sort of thing in his medical practice, but in his Gospel, he emphasizes that to become a follower of Christ, a person needs to repent. He gives multiple accounts of people who turned away from their former life to follow Jesus. For example, in his description of the ministry of John the Baptist, he says that John proclaimed a baptism of repentance, and gives three examples of what he told people to do. Everyone he baptized was expected to help the poor; tax collectors were told they shouldn't collect more than what people actually owed; and soldiers were not to extort money but be content with their pay. The story of Zacchaeus is another example of a transformed life. He was a corrupt and wealthy tax collector, but when he met Jesus, he repented. He sold half of his possessions to help the poor and repay those he had cheated.

Luke continues his focus on the theme of repentance in his account of Jesus' parables. In the parable of the barren fig tree, Jesus reveals that Israel is at a critical moment in history. He says that judgment is imminent. The nation has limited time to repent or face disaster.

Why a Fig Tree?

Grapes and figs were two of the most important crops in Israel's agricultural economy. After the spies made a reconnaissance of the land, they reported to Moses it was "a land flowing with milk and honey," a figure of speech for an abundance of food (Numbers 13:27). They brought back samples of grapes, pomegranates, and figs.

Fig trees grow large green leaves, which can provide shade from the hot sun in the Middle East, thus they are used as symbols of God's favor and his judgment. Peace and prosperity during the time of Solomon is described by saying each person sat under the shade of his own vine and fig tree (1 Kings 4:25). The prophets used figs as symbols of God's judgment. Isaiah warns the nations of God's fury: "The heavens above will melt away and disappear like a rolled-up scroll. The stars will fall from the sky like withered leaves from a grapevine, or shriveled figs from a fig tree (Isaiah 34:4 NLT; see also Jeremiah 5:17; Joel 1:7). It's a possibility that the leaves that Adam and Eve used to cover their nakedness after they ate the forbidden fruit were fig leaves. Maybe the fruit they ate was figs?

Figs also have medicinal value. When King Hezekiah was terminally ill, Isaiah ordered his physicians to prepare "a poultice of figs." They did as instructed, and Hezekiah was healed (2 Kings 20:7).

Amos, one of the prophets to Israel, was not a professional prophet. He was a sheep and cattle rancher and grower of sycamore fig trees in Tekoa, a small town in Judah, before the Lord called him as a prophet to the Northern Kingdom (Amos 7:14–15).

On the day after he had cleared the money changers out of the temple, Jesus cursed a barren fig tree to symbolize divine judgment on Israel (Matthew 21:18–22; cf. Mark 11:12–14, 20–21).

Jesus' disciples and the people following him would have fully understood the symbolism in a story about a barren fig tree.

Everyone Needs to Repent

The story is one of the parabolic lessons Jesus taught as he made his final journey to Jerusalem (Luke 9:51–19:27). It was the common belief that God blessed those who were good and punished those who were evil. Jesus refutes the traditional view that only bad people experience misfortune with two accounts of recent tragedies. He reminds them that Pilate brutally murdered a group of Galileans who were worshiping in the temple (Luke 13:1–3). In addition to human evil, innocent people often suffer from natural disasters. Eighteen Galileans were killed when the tower of Siloam collapsed (Luke 13:4–5). Jesus concludes both stories with a question and warning. He asks, "Were these people terrible sinners?" The expected answer is, "No!" And Jesus warns that everyone needs to repent or they too will perish.

Jesus told the story of the barren fig tree to emphasize the need for repentance and to warn of judgment for refusing his offer of the kingdom.

He Planted a Fig Tree

After he planted a fig tree, the farmer came repeatedly to look for fruit but didn't find any for three years. According to the law of Moses, after a fig tree had been planted, it was to be cultivated for three years to allow the tree to mature. The fruit in the fourth year was dedicated to the Lord. It was only in the fifth year that the fruit could be eaten (Leviticus 19:23–25). So the tree in the parable had been growing for at least six years, since the owner had been looking for figs for three years.

Because the tree was useless and taking up valuable space in his vineyard, the owner ordered his field hand to cut it down. The tree represents Israel, especially its religious leaders, who were as useless as the fruitless fig tree. However, the story takes a surprising turn at this point. The vinedresser asks for more time before destroying the tree. He says that he will take special care of it and make sure it gets plenty of fertilizer. Blomberg suggests, "The digging and spreading of manure may be an example of 'insult humor,' especially if the crowds realized Jesus had the Jewish leaders specially in view, but these details may just reflect natural horticulture practice."[1]

The harshness of judgment is moderated somewhat by the plea for mercy. Though Jesus is going to Jerusalem to fulfill his destiny on the cross, Israel still has time to repent. The parable is open-ended. We don't know what happened to the fig tree, but we do know what happened to the nation. They didn't repent and were destroyed by the Romans in AD 70.

If It Bears Fruit . . .

The immediate audience was Israel's religious leaders, who were spiritually barren. At the beginning of his ministry, John the Baptist used similar imagery to warn Israel of imminent judgment: "The ax is already at the root of the trees, and every tree that does not produce good fruit will be cut down and thrown into the fire" (Matthew 3:10).

The accounts of the worshipers who were murdered by Pilate and those killed by the collapse of the tower of Siloam suggest a broader application of the parable. Jesus' announcement of judgment and offer of mercy are critical considerations for each of us. The greatest failure in life is to reject Christ. Everyone needs a Savior, and Jesus is the only one who can save us. When arrested and interrogated by the Sanhedrin, Peter testified, "There is salvation in no one else! God has given no other name under heaven by which we must be saved" (Acts 4:12 NLT). And two stories that Jesus told to introduce the parable remind us that life is completely unpredictable. Tomorrow may be too late to make a decision about Christ.

We cannot save ourselves. The Bible is clear that salvation is by grace, but it is equally clear that a transformed life is evidence of genuine faith. James reinforces Jesus' warning when he writes, "So you see, faith by itself isn't enough. Unless it produces good deeds, it is dead and useless" (James 2:17 NLT). We must ask ourselves, "Does my life show evidence of genuine faith?" God does not expect us to be the best; he only asks that we do our best using whatever gifts and opportunities we have been given. We don't know how Onesimus, a runaway slave, had helped Paul, but Paul commended him to Philemon because he had become an asset in the work of the kingdom. "Formerly he was useless to you, but now he has become useful to you and to me" (Philemon 11). Tough question: "Am I useful or useless?"

|||||||||||||||||||||||||||||||||||||||||| **REFLECT** ||||||||||||||||||||||||||||||||||||||||||

1. Read 1 Kings 4:25; Micah 4:4; and Matthew 21:18–22. The prophets and Jesus often used grapes and figs to teach spiritual truths. What two figures of speech could be used today to teach spiritual truths? Why?

2. Read Luke 13:1–5. How do the stories about the murder of the Galileans and those who died when the tower of

Siloam collapsed refute the mistaken ideas that bad things only happen to bad people and that good people are protected from evil and misfortune?

   a. How do these stories emphasize the need to repent while there is still an opportunity?

   b. What unexpected tragedies have you experienced?

   c. How did these events cause you to rethink your priorities in life?

3. Read Luke 13:6–7. What do you think happened to Israel's religious leaders that made them unfruitful?

   a. What are some of the reasons that believers today can become unfruitful?

   b. What are some of the spiritual disciplines that you practice to be fruitful?

4. Read Galatians 5:22–25. What does it mean to be fruitful?

   a. What does Paul say we should do to produce the "fruit of the Spirit?"

   b. What does it mean to "walk in the Spirit"?

5. How has this parable encouraged you to be more faithful and fruitful in your life and service for Christ?

OPTIONAL

1. Read Luke 13:8 and Matthew 12:41–42. What does the vinedresser's request imply about the ministry of Christ?

   a. Why was Christ's offer of the kingdom Israel's last chance to enter it?

   b. Read 2 Peter 3:9. What does his request imply about the character of God?

   c. Why is it important that people not put off an opportunity to trust Christ as Savior?

2. Why is the failure to respond to God's call to trust Christ as Savior the greatest failure of all?

|||||||||||||||||||||||||||||||||| **Memory Verse** ||||||||||||||||||||||||||||||||||||

When the people heard this, they were cut to the heart and said to Peter and the other apostles, "Brothers, what shall we do?"

Peter replied, "Repent and be baptized, every one of you, in the name of Jesus Christ for the forgiveness of your sins. And you will receive the gift of the Holy Spirit."

Acts 2:37–38

The Vine
and the Branches

John 15:1–17

AUTHOR'S TAKEAWAY: *Staying connected is not an option; it's essential.*

In Northern California where our daughter lives, they grow grapes for making wine. Wine-making is a process that is far more complicated than I imagined. It takes time and a lot of effort to grow robust grapes that can be harvested and processed for wine. The ground must be cultivated; the vines fertilized and watered; and most of all, they must be pruned to maximize growth. People in first-century Palestine would have understood the process and easily identified with Jesus' teaching about a vine and its branches.

The background for this agricultural metaphor comes from the Old Testament. Psalm 80 is a lament. The psalmist uses two images to plead for restoration. God is Israel's shepherd, and they cry out to him to rescue them from their enemies (Psalm 80:1–7). Israel is also a vineyard that God planted in the land when he rescued them from Egypt (Psalm 80:8–18). The vineyard has been ravaged by enemies because God is no longer protecting his people. The Psalm

215

ends with a prayer for salvation that is answered by Jesus, who is the true vine (John 15:1–7). The same extended metaphor is used by Isaiah in the Song of the Vineyard (Isaiah 5:1–7). God planted Israel in the land, but when he looked for a harvest of sweet grapes, he found only bitter fruit. God will tear down the protective wall around Israel, and the vineyard will become desolate and useless. Later, Isaiah predicts that the Lord will restore the prosperity of the land (Isaiah 55:10–13).

When Jesus used the imagery of the vine and the branches, he was drawing on the Old Testament vineyard passages.

The Vine, the Gardener, and the Branches

When Jesus declared that he was the true grapevine, he changed the vineyard imagery. Using vineyard imagery, Jeremiah had warned Israel that God would punish them for rebellion (Jeremiah 2:21). Now, because of their failure, Jesus replaced Israel as the true vine. God was the gardener and Jesus' followers the branches. They have been cleansed because they have accepted the teaching of Jesus, "You are already clean because of the word I have spoken to you" (John 15:3). But to be fruitful, Jesus' followers must remain attached to him. The Father prunes fruitful branches so they will be even more fruitful, but cuts off unfruitful branches. They are burned because they are useless.

Remaining in Jesus

John uses the word *meno* ("remain" or "abide") to describe the dynamic relationship between Jesus and true believers. For John, the evidence of genuine faith is "remaining" in Jesus; the visible evidence of this dynamic relationship with Jesus is fruit-bearing. Fruitful disciples can be confident of answered prayer because their requests will conform to the will of God. And fruitful disciples will ultimately bring glory to the Father (John 15:7–8).

The key to remaining in Jesus (union with Christ) is to mirror the love and obedience relationship between Jesus and his Father. Fruitful disciples not only love Jesus, but are commanded to sacrificially love one another as Jesus has loved them. When they do what Jesus has commanded, they will experience joy—a sense of satisfaction that does not depend on circumstances (John 15:9–11).

Their union with Christ results in a new relationship. They are now friends, not slaves. Because they have this intimate relationship with Jesus, he will make known to them God's amazing plan of redemption—his plan to save the world through Jesus' sacrificial death on the cross. In anticipation of Jesus' death and resurrection, they are to bear fruit by proclaiming the gospel. This is why Jesus has chosen them and why they must love one another (John 15:12–17).

REFLECT

1. How has Jesus' teaching about the vine and branches helped you to better understand your relationships with the Father and Son?

2. As you think about your relationship with Christ, what can you do to be more fruitful?
   a. What needs pruning?
   b. What are some of the ways God prunes us to make us more fruitful?
   c. Why is pruning sometimes painful?

3. Why do you think Jesus emphasizes love and obedience as the keys for staying connected to him?

4. Jesus apparently teaches that our love is strengthened by obedience. What are some of the areas of your life that can be made stronger by obedience?

5. Read Matthew 22:34–40. How does Jesus' teaching in this passage complement his answer about the greatest commandment?

Jesus' teaching about the vine and branches is the basis for the concept of "union with Christ" that Paul and other writers explain as the fundamental union for all the benefits we have received as believers.

1. Read Galatians 2:20. How does Paul's testimony about what has happened to him because of his faith in Christ relate to Jesus' teaching about the vine and branches? How is your life different now than before you trusted Christ as Savior?

2. Read Romans 8:38–39. How does Paul's teaching inspire confidence in your relationship with God through Christ?

3. Read 1 John 3:16–17. What does John say is evidence of genuine love? Is there someone you can help?

|||||||||||||||||||||||||||||||| **Memory Verse** ||||||||||||||||||||||||||||||||

I am the vine; you are the branches. If you remain in me and I in you, you will bear much fruit; apart from me you can do nothing.

John 15:5

What Does God Expect of Me?

I have sometimes been asked, "Can you tell me what God expects of me?" That's an important question. My response is usually, "I can't, but Micah the prophet can." When people in ancient Israel were confused about morality and spirituality, Micah gave a clear and concise answer:

> He has shown you, O mortal, what is good.
> And what does the LORD require of you?
> To act justly, and to love mercy
> and to walk humbly with your God.
>
> Micah 6:8

It's obvious from his life and ministry that Jesus didn't come to perpetuate the spiritual stagnation and hypocrisy that plagued the religious establishment; he came to start a revolution—a spiritual revolution to establish the kingdom of God. Truths about the kingdom revolution are revealed in Jesus' parables. But Jesus' aim was to transform, not merely to inform. Yes, people needed to know about kingdom expectations, but they also needed to know how to live like subjects of the kingdom. Jesus' parables challenged people to think and live differently.

What did Jesus teach in his parables about the kingdom revolution? I think the words of Micah give us the answer.

1. He said that we should act justly. As the people of God, we should do what is right in our relationships with other people. Another word for justice is *righteousness*. Righteousness is an attribute of God and is transferred to us when we put our faith in Christ. But righteousness also refers to our relationships with people. The man did what was right when his friend asked for bread in the middle of the night for his unexpected guest. The parable of the widow and the unjust judge assures us that God is the exact opposite of the judge. God will surely act justly to those who come to him for help.

2. He said that we should love mercy. Mercy is the withholding of judgment, but also refers to acts of kindness. It's why we should help those in need. What could be more challenging than the parable of the good Samaritan?

3. He said that we should walk humbly with our God. I have difficulty defining humility, but fortunately Jesus' stories are filled with examples of humility. When Jesus saw the guests pushing and shoving to get the best seats at a wedding feast, he said to take the worst seats. The values in the kingdom are the opposite of the world. Those who exalt themselves will be humbled, and those who humble themselves will be exalted.

What does God expect of you and me? He wants us to act justly, love mercy, and walk humbly with our God. It's my hope and prayer that the study of the stories Jesus told will help you do that!

P.S. Of course not all of Jesus' parables can be put in those three categories. I identified only a few in the categories from Micah 6:8. For review, see how many you can place in each of the three categories.

Notes

Introduction

1. David Wenham, *The Parables of Jesus* (Downers Grove, IL: InterVarsity Press, 1989), 22–23.

2. Craig L. Blomberg, *Interpreting the Parables* (Downers Grove, IL: InterVarsity, 1999).

The Seed Growing Secretly

1. John D. Grassmick, "Mark" in *The Bible Knowledge Commentary* (Wheaton, IL: Victor Books, 1983), 121.

The Children in the Marketplace

1. Darrell Bock, *Jesus According to Scripture* (Grand Rapids, MI: Baker Publishing Group, 2017), 180.

Jesus and Beelzebul, the Strong Man, and Good and Bad Trees

1. *NLT Study Bible* (Carol Stream, IL: Tyndale, 2008), 1602.

The Wise and Foolish Virgins

1. Bock, *Jesus According to Scripture*, 350.

The Tower Builder and the Warring King

1. Blomberg, *Interpreting the Parables*, 283.

The Talents

1. William Barclay, *And Jesus Said: A Handbook on the Parables of Jesus* (Scotland: Church of Scotland Youth Committee, 1952), 171.

The Thief

1. Wenham, *The Parables of Jesus*, 76.

The Great Banquet

1. Kenneth Bailey, *Poet and Peasant and Through Peasant Eyes* (Grand Rapids, MI: Eerdmans, 1983) 100.

The Rich Man and Lazarus

1. Barclay, *And Jesus Said*, 93.

The Good Samaritan

1. Blomberg, *Interpreting the Parables*, 31.

The Helpless Widow and the Unjust Judge

1. Bailey, *Poet and Peasant and Through Peasant Eyes*, 131–32.
2. Bock, *Jesus According to Scripture*, 294.
3. Bock, 294.

The Pharisee and the Tax Collector

1. Simon J. Kistemaker, *The Parables: Understanding the Stories Jesus Told* (Grand Rapids, MI: Baker Books, 1980), 213.

The Friend at Midnight

1. BADG, A Greek-English Lexicon of the New Testament (Chicago: University of Chicago Press, 2000), 63.
2. Richard N. Longenecker, *The Challenge of Jesus' Parables* (Grand Rapids, MI: Eerdmans, 2000), 251.

The Lost Sheep and the Lost Coin

1. Blomberg, *Interpreting the Parables*, 181.

The Prodigal Son/the Loving Father

1. Barclay, *And Jesus Said*, 187.

The Unworthy Servant

1. Michael P. Knowles, "The Parable of the Unworthy Servant," quoted in Longenecker, *The Challenge of Jesus' Parables*, 297.

The Rich Fool

1. Blomberg, *Interpreting the Parables*, 268.

The Wicked Tenants

1. Barclay, *And Jesus Said: A Handbook on the Parables of Jesus*, 140.

The Barren Fig Tree

1. Blomberg, *Interpreting the Parables*, 269.

Dr. William H. Marty taught at Moody Bible Institute for thirty-seven years, focusing primarily on Old and New Testament survey. The fruit of his focus was published in *The Whole Bible Story*, a concise survey of God's unfolding plan of redemption. Dr. Marty has also authored *The World of Jesus*, a survey of the four hundred years between the Old and New Testaments, and *The Jesus Story*; and coauthored *A Quick-Start Guide to the Whole Bible*. His most recent publication is *102 Fascinating Bible Studies*, a book that provides a wealth of high-quality Bible studies for individual and small groups. Dr. Marty and his wife, Linda, live in Colorado near their grandchildren.

More from
Dr. William H. Marty

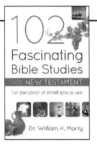

Organized by category, the 102 accessible Bible studies in this book span the New Testament, with topics including the temptations of Jesus, miracles, the words of Christ on the cross, and the Antichrist. Each study includes an introduction, Scripture references, and questions that open the door to lively discussion, reflection, or further investigation.

102 Fascinating Bible Studies on the New Testament

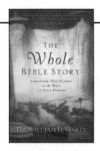

A seamless, straightforward, and chronological narrative of all the events in the Bible—without commentary—from creation to the New Testament church. *The Whole Bible Story* is perfect for new Christians looking to understand the overall flow of the Bible or for seasoned believers wanting a refresher course.

The Whole Bible Story

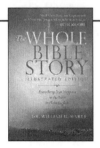

The sweeping narrative of the Bible presented in one engaging, easy-to-read story. It's the page-turning story of God's pursuit of you—one you'll want to read again and again. Includes full-color maps and photos.

The Whole Bible Story Illustrated Edition

◊ BETHANYHOUSE

Stay up to date on your favorite books and authors with our free e-newsletters. Sign up today at bethanyhouse.com.

 facebook.com/BHPnonfiction   @bethany_house_nonfiction

 @bethany_house

Made in the USA
Las Vegas, NV
08 January 2023

65229246R00125